J. J Smith

The Impending Conflict Between Romanism and Protestantism

in the United States

J. J Smith

The Impending Conflict Between Romanism and Protestantism
in the United States

ISBN/EAN: 9783337007997

Printed in Europe, USA, Canada, Australia, Japan

Cover: Foto ©Lupo / pixelio.de

More available books at **www.hansebooks.com**

THE

IMPENDING CONFLICT

BETWEEN

ROMANISM AND PROTESTANTISM

IN THE

UNITED STATES.

By REV. J. J. SMITH, D. D.

"How can two walk together except they be agreed?"

NEW YORK
E. GOODENOUGH, 122 NASSAU ST.
1871.

Entered according to Act of Congress, in the year one thousand eight
hundred and seventy-one,
By J. J. SMITH,
In the Office of the Librarian of Congress, at Washington.

JOHN J. REID, Printer, 43 Centre St., New York.

PREFACE.

This volume is intended to meet a public necessity, and is consequently a book for the times. It deals not with fiction, but with facts. It presents not theories, but inculcates action. Its origin is soon told. The attempt of Papists to expel the Bible from our Public Schools, and their outspoken denunciation of our entire common school system, elicited from me, about a year ago, a series of letters on our danger as a nation, from the aggressive spirit and policy of Romanism as being developed in our midst. These papers were first published in the Methodist Recorder. Several of my friends, whose mature judgments challenge my confidence, having expressed a wish, by letters and otherwise, to have those articles issued in book-form for more general circulation, constitute my apology, if apology be needed, for this publication.

The original letters have been enlarged, and nearly as many more chapters have been added, so as to cover most of the ground embraced in the questions involved. The reader will see in these pages that our controversy is with Popery as a *system*, which is, from its inherent nature, necessarily hostile to our free institutions, and not with its individual members, many of whom are justly esteemed for their private virtues and moral worth. As the present work deals with some of the most essential and vital issues of the day, it cannot fail at least to merit the attention of all classes, whatever may be the peculiar type of their religious convictions, or their political preferences.

That a most fearful conflict of antagonistic elements, (as embraced in the two widely diverging systems of Protestantism and Romanism,) is pending, which must inevitably culminate, sooner or later, in a fearful crisis, we believe to be absolutely certain. And since " to be forewarned is to be forearmed," my object in this undertaking is to awaken serious attention to the perils that surround us upon this subject. Our danger is imminent. Something needs to be done to stimulate the public mind and vitalize the moral forces of society to resist, by all lawful measures, the destructive tendencies of this vast foreign wave that is rolling in upon us and threatening to overwhelm us. I therefore earnestly entreat that all lovers of civil liberty, and religious toleration, of every name, will read the following pages, and reflect upon the signs of the times and the duties of the hour.

J. J. SMITH.

March 4th, 1871.

CONTENTS.

CHAPTER I.

Romanism essentially Antagonistic to Protestantism and our Free Institutions.

What is Meant by the Two Systems—Their Character—Necessary Antagonism—The Effect of the Dogma of Infallibility on the Question—Testimony of the "Catholic World"—Romanism fully Organized in our Midst—Warning of Dr. Wilie of Edinburgh 13-24

CHAPTER II.

The Influence of the Two Systems on Modern Civilization and Progress Contrasted.

Romanism is Conservativeism—Protestantism Progressive—What Macaulay says of Ireland, Switzerland and Germany—See Spain, Great Britain and Prussia—Victor Hugo's Testimony against Popery—See the Papal States—Gattini's Charge against the Popes—Lempriere's Statements as to the Workings of Popery in Mexico—M. Jonnés' and Mateucci's Testimonies—Statistics of Protestant and Catholic Countries in relation to Literature—In relation to Crime, etc....................................25-38

CHAPTER III.

Romish Aggression.

The Bible the Basis of our Institutions—Rome's Fixed Purpose to Expel it from our Schools—To Destroy the whole System—Her Struggles for Power—Her Intrigues and Influence in Political Circles—The Astounding Sums of Money secured by her Manipulations for Sectarian Purposes—Reflections—Their Aggression in other Places—The Destruction of our Schools their Object........................39–49

CHAPTER IV.

The Avowed Purposes of Rome in the United States.

Testimony of the "Catholic World" and other Catholic Publications—Startling Declarations of her Bishops—Hostility to our Free Institutions admitted and proclaimed.................................50–57

CHAPTER V.

Further Cause of Alarm from Popery.

Their rapid Increase in the United States—Statistics—Emigration—Their Sectarian Schools—These admitted by themselves to be vastly Inferior to Protestant Schools—The Result of Protestants sending their Children to Roman Catholic Schools—The Compactness of the Papal System the Secret of its Power—The Intriguing Fraternity of Jesuits in our midst..58–69

CHAPTER VI.

Romanists versus Public Schools.

Their Opposition Persistent and Determined—Their Hostility Proclaimed—Their Opposition to them in Holland—Their Policy here Destructive to the whole System—We can never Submit to it.......70–77

CHAPTER VII.

Romanism versus Bible.

Pope Gregory VII. and Clement XI. against the Common Use of the Bible—Also the Councils of Toulouse

Contents. vii

and Trent—Quesnel's Testimony—Clement XI.'s Reply—Persecution of the Waldenses for Bible-reading—Pope Pius VII. and Leo XII.—Gregory XVI. against Bible Societies—Dr. Murry's and Clark's Testimonies of the Scarceness of the Bible in Rome—Incidents of Hostility to Bible-reading in Ireland and Mexico—Pope Gregory XVI. in 1844 against Circulating the Scriptures—The Circulation of Catholic Bibles without Note or Comment Forbidden by Benedict XIV.—Roman Catholic Bibles Burned in Chili by Romish Priests—Romanists have no Bible Societies......................78-93

CHAPTER VIII.

Our Public Schools a Necessity to the Perpetuity of our Free Institutions.

Our Danger from Ignorance—Ignorance the Fruitful Source of Crime—Intelligence the Basis of National Safety—Common Schools never a greater Necessity than now—Horace Mann on Common Schools—Their Necessity in the Light of Emigration—Education should be Enforced by Law—Prussian System—Statistics in United States............94-104

CHAPTER IX.

A Moral Element of Instruction is Essential to the Success of our Public School System and the Welfare of the Nation.

This, Recognized by the Founders of our Government—Chief Justice Shaw's Statement—Our Government Based on Morality—Morality Essential to its Existence—The Bible a Necessity—M. Cousin's Report—The Sad Experience of France in Rejecting the Bible—What Rousseau said—Astounding Declarations of a Romanist—Decision of an English Court—Professor Stowe's Report—Drs. Clark and Bud-

ington's Testimony—The Necessity of Teaching
Morality in our Public Schools 105–121

CHAPTER X.

The Bible a Suitable Book for our Public Schools.

As a Moral Instructor the Bible has no Equal--The Character of its Parables, etc.—Rousseau's Confession of its Sublimity—Sir W. Jones' Eulogy on the Bible—What the Bible has done—Our Duty to Teach it to our Children......................122–128

CHAPTER XI.

The Literary Character of the Bible an Additional Reason why its Use should be Continued in our Public Schools.

It is the Most Ancient of Histories—Prof. Huxley's Admission—Its Stories of Interest and Beauty—Daniel Webster's Testimony—Its Biographies, Maxims, Songs, etc.—Quotations from R. H. Dana and Dr. Nevens—Poetry and Eloquence of the Bible—Its Influence on Science—Dr. Todd's Statement, etc....... 129–138

CHAPTER XII.

Our Public Schools are not made Sectarian by the Use of the Bible as Charged by Romanists.

The Bible not a Sectarian Book—The Bearing of the Practice of Courts of Justice upon this Question—King James' Translation of the Bible not a Sectarian Translation—Made mostly by Catholics—A Catholic's Opinion of it—Opinions of Others—The Douay Version purely Sectarian—Examples of this Fact—Catholics are not Satisfied to have their own Version in the Schools—They mean to Break Down our School System......................139–149

Contents.

CHAPTER XIII.

Our Public School System is not subversive of the rights of Romanists.

Papists treated just as all others are treated.—Majorities and minorities.—Individual preferences must yield to the wish of Society.—Without this Society could not exist as such.—Dr. Wayland's position.—Protestants have Consciences as well as Catholics.—Catholics have Liberty to do as they please.—What a Court says upon the subject.—Papists' demand unreasonable..................150–159

CHAPTER XIV.

Shall we consent to Banish the Bible from our Public Schools to please Romanists or any other Sect?

As a people we are under great obligations to the Bible.—The demand of Papists absurd.—What a Catholic says of Protestants and the Bible.—What is involved in banishing the Bible from our Schools.—Gen. Pilsbury's Report.—To banish the Bible from our Schools will not save them.—If we banish the Bible we must also banish other books and studies.—Shall we array ourselves against the Bible?................................160–170

CHAPTER XV.

Why Romanists are Opposed to the Bible.

Because the Bible Opposes their System—their Pagan rites—Image Worship.—Council of Trent on Image Worship.—Douay Bible.—Their expediency to get rid of the Command that forbids Image Worship.—Their System of Image Worship and Heathen Idolatry the same.—Their reason for the practice the same as Heathens................171–179 x *Contents.*

CHAPTER XVI.

The Paganism of Popery—The Celibacy of the Clergy Unscriptural and Pagan.

The astounding Criminality of the Priests to which it has led.—Their present Character at Rome.—Celibacy of the Clergy not in the Bible—not in the Primitive Church—a Pagan institution.—Why the Church of Rome adopted it............ 180–186

CHAPTER XVII.

The Paganism of Rome the Secret of her Opposition to the Bible.

The Holy Water.—Its supposed Virtue.—Ridiculous uses.—Its efficacy as declared by Papal authority.—It is not in the Bible.—It is borrowed from Pagans.—The striking similarity between its preparation and use by Heathens and Romanists....187–195

CHAPTER XVIII.

Paganism of Popery.—The Candle Burning.

Her constant use of Candles.—How Consecrated.—Their supposed Virtue.—Candlemass not of the Bible.—Its Pagan origin indisputable.—So acknowledged by Pope Innocent III.—Candle-burning gross Idolatry................ 196–202

CHAPTER XIX.

The Paganism of Popery.—The Origin of Monkery.

Her Monastic Institutions.—Their Pagan origin.—Father Huc's testimony.—Another Jesuit's testimony.—When and how Monkery came into the Church.—Roman Penance.—Its Origin.—Not of the Bible.—Their false translation of $M\varepsilon\tau\alpha\nu οια$.20–211

Contents. xi

CHAPTER XX.

The Paganism of Popery.—Purgatory and Canonized Saints.

Her doctrine of Purgatory—not of the Bible.—Its Origin.—A Papist's admission.—How it came to be adopted.—Supplication to departed Saints.—Canonized Saints in the Romish Church, what deified heroes were among the Greeks and Romans.—The Virgin Mary to Catholics what Diana was to the Ephesians.—Why so many are Canonized.—Rome's many other Pagan customs............212-221

CHAPTER XXI.

Roman Despotism.

The astounding utterances of Popes.—Their tyranny over Kings.—Their cruel Mandates.—Their haughty assumptions of being above all Law...........223-230

CHAPTER XXII.

Rome still Despotic.

Popery unchanged.—Testimony of Catholics themselves on the subject.—Pope Pius IX. against Reforms in Austria.—Hostility of the Romish Hierarchy to Republicanism in Mexico—to Reforms in Italy.—The Pope's Sympathy with our late Rebellion.—The Riot in New York a Catholic Riot.—The Emperor of France and the Pope.—Popery in Spain.—The recent Papal Government at Rome.—What the Pope's subjects thought of it.—Outspoken hostility of American Romish Priests and Bishops to Popular Governments.............231-246

CHAPTER XXIII.

Romanism an Intolerant and Persecuting Power.

Decision of the Council of Toledo.—Council of Lateran.—Decision of Popes.—The Oath of a Jesuit. —Bishop's Oath.—Persecution of the Waldenses. —Vaudois in France.—Decree of Paul IV.—Inquisition.—Motley's account of its doings.—Rome's Cruelty.—Massacre of St. Bartholomew.—How received at Rome.—Massacre in Ireland.........247-266

CHAPTER XXIV.

Popish Persecutions of Bible Readers in Maderia.

Scarcity of the Bible.—The People's Ignorance.—Dr. Kalley furnishes them with Catholic Bibles.—The Priests are alarmed.—Bibles denounced.—Persecutions commence. Violent Measures adopted.— The terrible suffering of the Bible readers.—Their flight from the Island......................267-274

CHAPTER XXV.

Rome still a Persecutor in Spain.

Her teachings.—Her recent acts of Intolerance and Persecution in Hungary.—Madeira.—Ecuador.— Nicaragua.—The effect of the dogma of Papal Infallibility on this question.—Popery's cruel spirit as inculcated in her teachings.—The Ma!or curse, or *Anathama Maranatha* recently pronounced on Victor Emanuel.—The Anathema pronounced on all Protestants Thursday before Easter.—The baseness of the act.............................275-288

THE IMPENDING CONFLICT.

CHAPTER I.

Romanism essentially Antagonistic to Protestantism and our Free Institutions.

WE do not mean by Romanism the membership of the Roman Catholic communion, for many of these are undoubtedly, at heart, in entire sympathy and harmony with our free institutions; but we mean by Romanism the Romish hierarchy, consisting of priests, bishops, archbishops, and cardinals, with the Pope at their head, governing, controlling, and directing the entire membership in all things in the most absolute manner.

We mean by Protestantism, not that body of Christian believers who acted with Luther in 1529 in protesting against the tyranny, intolerance, and gross corruptions of the Romish Church, and who also entered their solemn protest against the decree of Charles V. and the Diet of Spires; but we mean that system of religious truths and principles embodied in the earnest protest of Christ and his apostles against the intolerance, formalism, hypocrisy and tyranny of the Pharisees. The Reformation was but the re-establishment of primitive Christianity or Protestantism, by vigorously maintaining the great central principles of human equality, individual responsibility, and internal purity. Protestantism is therefore an earnest protest against Roman idolatry, intolerance, despotism, etc.

That there is a distinct antagonism between the two great systems of religious faith, as embodied in Protestantism and Romanism, every body knows, who knows any thing about the history of the past or the experience of the present. All, however, do not alike understand that this antagonism is by no means necessarily owing to a want of kindly feelings upon the part of their respective adherents, but the unavoidable result of the antagonistic nature of the essentials of the two systems. It is not in the nature of things that they should harmonize. They adhere to contrary principles that necessarily involve a moral conflict. The two systems possess, comparatively speaking, but few points of agreement, while their differences are numerous and fundamental. These are to be traced back to the great central idea that lies at the foundation of each system, and which gives to each its individual form and character. The Protestant central idea is that "the Bible is the only rule, and the all sufficient rule of faith and practice." The Romanists, on the other hand, hold that the Bible is *not* the only rule or a sufficient rule; but that the writings of the Fathers, the decretals of the Popes, and the decrees of Councils are necessary to make up the rule for faith and practice. It is owing to this absurd dogma that so much that is found in the Romish Church is not only not in the Bible, but in direct violation of its spirit and its teachings. Hence it is that Rome presents to the world the strange incongruous medley of something of Christianity, a part of Judaism, and more of Paganism.

It is therefore not strange that the two systems should not harmonize. Their antagonism is inevitable. "What communion hath light with darkness? What concord hath Christ with Belial? or what part hath he that believeth with an infidel?" "He that is not with me is against me, and he that gathereth not with me scattereth abroad," is the emphatic language of Christ. And again, "How can two walk together except they be agreed?" As well might we attempt to mix oil and water as to harmonize such discordant elements as are found in the two systems.

Protestantism seeks by the organization of Bible Societies and by all available means to put the Bible in possession of all men; Romanism forbids and prohibits to the extent of its power the circulation of the Scriptures among the people. Protestantism declares Jesus Christ to be the true and only head of the church, as Paul affirms " *Christ is the head of the Church ;*" Romanism says the Pope is the head of the church. Protestantism puts the Bible foremost in her worship ; Romanism makes the mass the principal thing. Romanism thunders its excommunications against all who abandon its superstitious rites, and declares there is no salvation outside the pales of her communion, while Protestantism teaches and holds that Jesus Christ is the Saviour of all men, especially of them that believe, wherever found. Romanism teaches that the efficacy of religious worship consists in external forms and pompous ceremonies; Protestantism that it consists in worshiping God in spirit and in truth. Romanism proceeds from the visible church (the Papacy) to the invisible church ; Protestantism from the invisible, (the true body of Christ,) to the visible. Romanism works from without, and from the general to the particular—Protestantism from within, and from the individual to the general. Romanism seeks to bring all men into subjection to the church. Protestantism aims to bring all into obedience to Christ. Protestantism is an earnest protest against tyranny ; Romanism aims at universal despotism. Protestantism is tolerant, giving to every man the right to worship God according to the dictates of his own conscience; Romanism is intolerant, dogmatical and proscriptive. Protestantism has but one Mediator, Jesus Christ; Romanism has many in the form of canonized saints. Protestantism goes directly to Christ for salvation; Romanism goes to the Virgin Mary. Romanism seeks by all available means to subject the mind to the priesthood—Protestantism seeks to bring all in subjection to Christ; the former is a system invented for the glory and aggrandizement of itself, in which the sacerdotal element is dominant and essential, the latter a system in which the glory of God and the good of souls are dominant; the former makes the Pope the lawful source of all political power, and the custodian of all political rights, the latter the popular will.

The very element of Romanism is dogmatism. Its character and spirit are necessarily against Protestantism and Republican institutions. Its system at best is but a baptized system of Paganism, or a materialized scheme that chains humanity to earth, instead of lifting it to heaven. It debases the mind by substituting senseless dogmas in the place of reason, until a blind fanaticism and superstition become the governing forces of the will. Protestantism, on the other hand, seeks to train the individual to think for himself, to use his own mind, to judge for himself, and to take the Bible as the man of his counsel.

Of all the forms of despotism under the sun, both in the aggregate and concrete, either in ancient or modern times, none can claim greater perfection than Romanism. This hierarchy has, accordingly, not only claimed the divine right to rule the nations of the earth according to its own pleasure, but it has tyrannized over mankind politically and ecclesiastically in the most shameful manner. The most ancient and sacred rights of communities it has trampled in the very dust, as it has deposed emperors, given away kingdoms, excommunicated rulers, and deprived whole nations of religious rites.

Can any one doubt that such a system as is embodied in Romanism, which denies a man the right of private judgment, the right of conscience, the right to worship in the manner that he may judge best, the right to think, and the right to speak, can be other than destructive to our free institutions?

The delusive hope that has been cherished by many that Rome was becoming ashamed of her past arrogant assumptions and tyrannical practices, has been forever dissipated by the recent absurd dogma of Papal infallibility. By this shameful act the present is irretrievably linked with the past. Progress, which in her case was well nigh hopeless before, is impossible now. It will not do any longer to say that Romanism is modernized and adapted to Democratic institutions. Between Rome and our free institutions there is and ever must be an " irrepressible conflict"—an irreconcilable hostility. This fact is even admitted by Catholics themselves. The *Catholic World* of April last, says:

" The difference between Catholics and Protestants is not a difference in details or particulars only, but a *difference* in *principle*. Catholicity must be taught as a whole, in its unity and its integrity, or it is not taught at all. It must everywhere be *all* or nothing. It is not a simple theory of truth or a collection of doctrines ; it is an organism, a living body, living and operating from its own central life, and is necessarily one and indivisible, and *cannot have any thing in common with any other body.*"

Again, from the same paper, we have the following:

" For ourselves, we do not pretend that the church is or ever has been tolerant. She is *undeniably intolerant* in her own order, as the law, as truth is intolerant, though she does not necessarily require the State to be tolerant. *She certainly is opposed to what the nineteenth century calls religious liberty.* The nineteenth century may not be able to understand it, or, if understanding it, to accept it ; yet it is true that the spiritual is the superior, and the law of the temporal. The supremacy belongs in all things of right to God, represented on earth by the church or the spiritual order. The temporal has no rights, no legitimacy save as subordinated by the spiritual."

In the preceding extracts from one of their leading journals, we have not only the distinct affirmation that Romanism is " different in principle" and must be " all or nothing," but that " she is undeniably intolerant," and " certainly is opposed to what the nineteenth century calls religious liberty."

Let Protestants who have heretofore been sleeping over this fearful, seething, surging volcano of Romanism, ponder these and kindred utterances of papists in reference to the terrible character of their own system, and their avowed purposes to subjugate our country to their control. Let them reflect that this despotic hierarchy is already fully organized in our midst. That the Pope has set up over us a large number of bishops and arch-bishops. That these have bowed with deferential awe to the blasphemous dogma of Papal infallibility, and proclaim themselves ready to do the Pope's bidding.

Of the anti-republican character of the Papal system there is not a doubt. Her whole past and present history is replete with demonstrations of this fact. If in this land she has seemed to be indifferent, it is because she lacks the necessary power. The tiger, caged or asleep, is a tiger still. We are not to fancy that, because he lies with half-shut eyes and sheathed claws, that his nature is changed to that of the lamb. So with Rome. She boasts that she changes not. That what she is in the Papal States, she is every where. That what she has done in former ages she has the will to do again. She proclaims aloud that modern civilization as a whole, including political freedom, self-government, secular education, etc., are damnable heresies, that are to be opposed and overthrown wherever practicable.

Now can any one fail to see, that in the very nature of things, a terrible conflict of opposing principles is pending between the two systems in these United States? Such are the antagonistic characters, conflicting elements, and opposing forces of the two systems, that a perilous rupture is inevitable at no distant day. We have already had some little experience as a nation in the impossibility of harmonizing, or even avoiding a terrible conflict between essentially different systems, in our late rebellion. But then, as now, there was the constant cry, "no danger," resounding through all the North, until we were suddenly awakened from our delusive dream of peace and security, by the crashing thunders of rebel artillery. If a conflict could not be avoided with our own kindred, speaking the same language, sustaining the same relations to the general government, and holding the same religious faith, because they sought to maintain an anti-republican institution in their midst, how do we expect to avoid a conflict with Romanism, that every year is becoming relatively stronger, and which is under the control of a foreign despot, and whose every essential feature is at war with every essential principle of our government? It is impossible. Secular dominion is her aim. Her dogmatic arrogance, her despotic nature, and her unbounded ambition, are even now arming her with the determination to take the offensive, and hurl her whole weight with force and energy against our Republican institutions. She necessarily hates Democracy here as everywhere else, and is accordingly preparing for the struggle. Says Dr. Wilie of Edinburgh:

"It is plain that the issue of this war, to the Papacy, must be one of two things, complete annihilation or unbounded dominion. Rome must be all that she ever was and more, or cease to be. Europe is not wide enough to hold both the Old Papacy and the Young Democracy; and one or other must go to the wall. Matters have gone too far to permit of the contest being ended by a truce or compromise; the battle must be fought out. If the Democracy shall triumph, a fearful retribution will be exercised on a church which has proved herself to be essentially sanguinary and despotic; and if the Church shall overcome, the Revolution will be cut up root and branch. It is not for victory then, but for life that both parties now fight. The gravity of the juncture and the eminent peril in which the Papacy is placed, will probably spirit it on to some desperate attempt. Half measures will not save it at such a crisis as this. To retain only the traditions of its power, and to practice the comparatively tolerant policy which it has pursued for the past half century, will no longer either suit its purpose or be found compatible with its continued existence. It must become the living, dominant Papacy once more. In order that it may exist it must reign. We may therefore expect to witness some combined and vigorous attempt on the part of Popery to recover its former dominion. It has studied the genius of every people; it has fathomed the policy of every government; it knows the principles of every sect, and school, and club—the sentiments and feelings of almost every individual; and with its usual tact and ability it is attempting to control and harmonize these various conflicting elements so as to work out its own ends." Again: "These two tremendous forces, Democracy and Catholicism, poise one another, and neither can reign so long as both exist. But who can tell how soon the equilibrium may be destroyed? Should the balance preponderate in favor of the Catholic element; should Popery succeed in bringing over from the Infidel and Democratic camp a sufficient number of converts to enable her to crush her antagonist, the supremacy is again in her hands. With Democracy collapsed, with the State exhausted and owing its salvation to the Church, and with a priesthood burning to avenge the disasters and humiliations of three centuries—wo to Europe—the darkest page of its history would be yet to be written."

What Rome is seeking to accomplish in Europe, she is seeking with greater energy to accomplish here.

We do not, however, believe that this country is destined to be surrendered to the Pope, or that the Romish hierarchy will ever be able to establish their supremacy upon the ruins of our free institutions. But we firmly believe that a great struggle is at hand, that hard fighting is to be done—it cannot be otherwise. The most stupendous questions are involved in the contest, and the American people should at once prepare themselves to meet it as best they can ; to meet it firmly and boldly as they have met in former days the enemies of our free institutions, using the means that Providence has given them, and trusting in the God of battles for victory.

Nay, the conflict has already begun. A deep laid conspiracy has already been formed against one of the cherished institutions of the American people, the very bulwark of our national life, our Public Schools. Already are heard the distant muttering thunders of the coming storm. A black and wrathful cloud is already seen darkening the horizon which threatens our country with utter desolation. And what adds greatly to our danger, and is itself a source of alarm, the majority of our fellow citizens are asleep upon this subject. They fail utterly to discern the signs of the times. Amid the astounding declarations and developments of Romanism in our land, they utterly fail to recognize Popery as the implacable foe of civil and religious liberty.

CHAPTER II.

The Influence of the two systems on Modern Civilization and Progress, contrasted.

THE essential difference in nature and the antagonistic character of the two systems, Protestantism and Romanism, are not more distinctly visible to the mind than the marked difference of their influences upon modern civilization, human progress, and all that which is essential to the welfare of our race. No fact is better substantiated than this, that the Romish hierarchy, with the Pope at its head, has arrayed itself against civil liberty, against freedom of conscience, against an untrammeled press, against the spirit of scientific inquiry, in a word, against all the live forces and tendencies of modern society. It has outraged the intelligence of the nineteenth century by its stubborn adherence to the musty and cobwebed dogmas of the dark ages. While it is resolved to learn nothing by experience, it has also resolved to hold all mankind back from progress. By the decisions of its Councils, and the decretals of its Popes, it has most effectually divorced the Romish Church from the development, intelligence, and rapid progress of the society of the present age. Under its corrupting reign, its votaries though full-grown are mentally and morally dwarfed, and lying in swaddling clothes, with no chance for improvement. Under its influence society languishes and dies.

Pope Pius IX. has spent more than twenty years in denouncing civilization and human progress, and as if forever hereafter to block effectually the wheels of advancement, has caused the dogma of Papal infallibility to be proclaimed, by which the ignorance, despotism, and superstitions of the dark ages are to be glorified.

The reverse of all this is Protestantism. Hence it has been most prominently allied with the material success and prosperity of nations for the last three hundred years. Protestantism rather than Romanism, has been the mighty agent that has elevated the nations by stimulating thrift, enterprise, culture, refinement, civilization, and morality. Protestantism is the great moral pioneer of the world. Protestant countries stand in the front rank of nations; Roman countries lag in the back ground. Wherever Protestantism has secured a firm footing, there wealth is most abundant, industry most apparent, education most general, happiness greatest, and intelligence highest. The difference between Protestant countries and Roman Catholic countries is too palpable to be denied by any one. The great historian and philosopher, Macaulay, in speaking of the manifest superiority of Protestantism over Romanism says, "that when in Ireland you pass from a Catholic to a Protestant county, in Switzerland from a Catholic to a Protestant canton, or in Germany from a Catholic to a Protestant state, you feel you are passing from a lower to a higher civilization." As great as the difference is in thrift, enterprise, intelligence, and culture, the contrast is still greater in reference to morals.

"*Nearly the whole of the Teutons are Protestants*, and there has long been in operation a fixed law by which the Protestant powers have been rising in the world, while those under Papal influence have been on the decline. There are certain great crises in the history of nations and of individuals when, on their conduct for a comparatively brief period, their whole future destiny turns. This, as a rule, happens when truth and error are, in the providence of God, presented to them side by side, and they are asked to state which they prefer. France rejected Protestantism and embraced Popery, and she has been smarting for her choice ever since. When the so-called 'Invincible Armada' threatened the overthrow of Protestant England, Spain could boast of 43,000,000 inhabitants; she has now only 14,000,000. Heaven has stricken her in her first-born as it smote the Egyptians. With the growth of Protestantism in Ireland, prosperity is dawning upon that unhappy land, yet within our times Ireland has lost upwards of 2,500,000 inhabitants, more than one-third of the whole. Left under the dominion of the Papacy, the logical demonstration is that these countries will become, like the deserted Palmyra, Thebes, or Memphis, howling wildernesses, residence for the toad, the bat, the wolf, and the serpent.

"Looking at Protestant nations, Great Britain had 10,800,000 when the Armada came; she has now 32,000,000 in these islands. Besides this, she has largely peopled America, India, and Australia, New Zealand, and other islands of the South. She has centupled her wealth; she has seen her children grow from ten millions to ten times ten millions, and has spread the Bible over all the world.

"Look at Prussia. Only a century and a half ago the title of the King of Prussia was first assumed. But Protestant truth was offered to it and accepted, and, amid struggles, it spread. Blessed with a succession of able Electors, and then of Kings equally distinguished, Prussia became a formidable kingdom. It is thus a fact that the Protestant powers of Europe have for three centuries been rising, while those enslaved by the Papacy have been sinking into deeper depths."*

Such are the opposite results of the two systems upon national growth and prosperity.

When Romish priests, a few years since, endeavored to regain the entire instruction and control of the national schools in France, from which they had twice been expelled, Victor Hugo brilliantly exposed their unfitness for the position from their uniform opposition to the progress of modern ideas, when he boldly said:

"Ah, we know you. We know the clerical party. It is an old party. This is it which has found for the truth those two marvellous supporters, ignorance and error! This it is which forbids to science and genius the going

* *Primitive Methodist, England.*

beyond the missal, and which wishes to cloister thought in dogmas. Every step which the intelligence of Europe has taken has been in spite of it. This it is which caused Prinelli to be scourged for having said that the stars would not fall. This it is which put Campanella seven times to the torture, for having affirmed that the number of worlds was infinite. This it is which persecuted Harvey for having proved the circulation of the blood. In the name of Jesus, it shut up Galileo. In the name of St. Paul, it imprisoned Christopher Columbus. To discover a law of the heavens was an impiety.

"For a long time you have tried to put a gag upon the human intellect. You wish to be the masters of education. And there is not a poet, not an author, not a philosopher, not a thinker, that you accept. All that has been written, found, dreamed, deduced, inspired, imagined, invented by genius, the treasure of civilization, the venerable inheritance of generations, the common patrimony of knowledge, you reject.

"And you claim the liberty of teaching. Stop, be sincere; let us understand the liberty which you claim. It is the liberty of *not* teaching. You wish us to give you the people to instruct. Very well. Let me see your pupils. Let us see those you have produced. What have you done for Italy? What have you done for Spain? For centuries you have kept in your hands, at your discretion, at your schools, these two great nations, illustrious among the illustrious. What have you done for them? I am going to tell you. Thanks to you, Italy, whose name no man who thinks can any longer pronounce without an inexpressible filial emotion; Italy, mother of genius and of nations, which has spread over the universe all the most brilliant marvels of poetry and the arts; Italy, which has taught mankind to read, now knows not how to read! Yes, Italy is, of all the

States of Europe, that where the smallest number of natives know how to read.

"Spain, magnificently endowed; Spain, which received from the Romans her first civilization, from the Arabs her second civilization, from Providence, in spite of you, a world—America; Spain, thanks to you, to your yoke of stupor, which is a yoke of degradation and decay, Spain has lost this secret power, which it had from the Romans; this genius of art, which it had from God; and in exchange for all that you have made it lose, it has received from you the Inquisition.

"The Inquisition, which certain men of the party try to-day to re-establish; which has burned on funeral pile millions of men; the Inquisition, which disinterred the dead to bury them as heretics; which declared the children of heretics even to the second generation, infamous and incapable of any public honors, excepting only those who shall have denounced their fathers; the Inquisition, which, while I speak, still holds in the Papal library the manuscripts of Galileo, sealed under the Papal signet! These are your masterpieces. This fire, which we call Italy, you have extinguished. This colossus, that you call Spain, you have undermined. The one is in ashes, the other in ruins. This is what you have done for two great nations. What do you wish to do for France?"

Such priests are now forcing upon the American people the question of sustaining or abandoning our common school system. It is well to review the record of Rome in the past, that we may know what to expect of it in the future.

We are assured by travelers and by reliable statistics, that among all civilized nations, there are nowhere to be found such ignorance and superstition, such poverty and degradation as exist in the Papal States. Rome is behind all the rest of Europe in literature, science, thought, progress, and civilization. Here for centuries there has been no great movement in social elevation, in political reforms, or in moral improvement, but an earnest and solemn protest from the Popes against intellectual advancement, political reforms, free institutions, and religious toleration.

Gattini (Italian M.P.), in speaking of the Papacy, brings out the following important facts bearing upon this subject. He says:

"Civilization asks what share the Papacy has taken in its work. Is it the press? Is it electricity? Is it steam? Is it chemical analysis? Is it free trade? Is it self-government? Is it the principle of nationality? Is it the proclamation of the rights of man? Of the liberty of conscience? Of all this the Papacy is the negation. Its culminating points are Gregory I., who, like Omar, burnt libraries; Gregory VII., who destroyed a moiety of Rome and created the temporal sovereignty; Innocent III., who founded the Inquisition; Boniface IX., who destroyed the last remains of municipal liberty in Rome; Pius VII., who committed the same wrong in Bologna; Alexander VI., who established the censorship of books; Paul III., who published the bull for the establishment of the Jesuites; Pius V., who covered Europe with burning funeral piles; Urban VIII., who tortured Galileo; and Pius IX., who has given us the modern *Syllabus.*"

It would be difficult to conceive of a more

damaging record than that of the Popes in the foregoing; and yet that spirit of antagonism to progress is every where where Popery is dominant.

"The Mexican Church, as a Church," says Lempriere, "fills no mission of virtue, no mission of morality, no mission of mercy, no mission of charity. Virtue cannot exist in its pestiferous atmosphere. The code of morality does not come within its practice. It knows no mercy, and no emotion of charity ever nerves the stony heart of the priesthood, which, with an avarice that has no limit, filches the last penny from the diseased and dying beggar; plunders the widows and orphans of their substance, as well as their virtue; and casts such a horoscope of horrors around the death-bed of the dying millionaire that the poor, superstitious wretch is glad to purchase a chance for the safety of his soul, by making the Church the heir of his treasures."

And what the Roman Catholic Church has done for poor down-trodden Mexico, she is ready to do for us.

In the kingdom of Spain where she established the Inquisition, and where her will was law, not until after the lapse of one-third of the present century, was there but *one* newspaper published in that country! "Yes, one miserable government gazette, was the sole channel through which 12,000,000 or 14,000,000 of people, spread over a vast territory, were to be supplied with information on the momentous af-

Influence of Popery. 33

fairs of their own country, and the whole external world."*

General education was entirely unknown, and consequently the most deplorable state of ignorance and its attendant, superstition, prevailed on every side. According to returns made in the year 1803, and it is believed but little change has been made since; exclusive of those brought up in convents and monasteries, only *one* in every 346 of the population were receiving any education at all.

M. Jonnés, who may be supposed to know as much about this subject as any one, estimates that the present number of children in schools in the whole of Spain, is not over 43,000 out of over 1,500,000 of children of school age, or about one in thirty-five. Such is the result of Romanism in that priest-ridden country.

In 1861, Professor Mateucci, Secretary of State for Public Instruction, in a report to the legislative body, made the following mournful statement concerning the ignorance of Italians:

"In Lombardy and Piedmont (always and in everything the most advanced provinces of Italy), little more than three persons in one hundred were able to read and write; a few more could spell; but, making all allowance possible, ninety persons out of one hundred did not even know their letters nor the arithmetical figures. In Central Italy, that is, in the Grand Duchy of Tuscany,

* National Education, Vol. II., p. 136.

the Duchies of Parma, Modena, Lucca, and in the Aemilia, it was much worse, yet they were well off in comparison with Southern Italy, *beginning with Rome down to Sicily: for here not one in one hundred had received any mental training.*"

It should be borne in mind, that this gross darkness exists in a region which contains one-third of the Episcopates in all the Roman Catholic world. It possesses 235 Archbishops and Bishops; priests by tens of thousands; 625 monasteries; 537 nunneries, the members of the monastic order being over 73,000; and 288 Episcopal seminaries. All these have hitherto had charge of Italy's education, and are sustained by onerous taxation; and yet nearly *ninety-nine hundredths of the population intrusted to their care can neither read nor write.*

There is not only a greater amount of ignorance where Romanism is predominant as compared with Protestant countries, and that ignorance in proportion to the completeness of her jurisdiction; but there is also, as might be expected, a greater percentage of crime in Roman Catholic countries than in Protestant countries.

A certain writer not long since copied, as he informs us, from "*the most reliable authority,*" the following statistics which were published in the London *Examiner*, from which they were copied by the *Christian Intelligencer*. These statistics show the relative proportion of crime between Protestant and Roman countries. The proportion of murders to the population is as follows: In England 1 in every 178,000; in Holland 1 in every 163,000; in Prussia 1 in every 100,000; in Spain 1 in every 4,113; in Naples 1 in every 2,750; and in Rome and the Papal States 1 in every 750.

Protestant England, in this respect is the best, and Papal Rome the worst. So there are 237 murders in Rome in a given population to where there is one in England in the same population.

The same authority shows conclusively the superior state of morals among Protestants in relation to the sanctity of the marriage relation as contrasted with Romanists. The following figures show the percentage of illegitimate births: In London 4; in Paris 48; in Brussels 53; in Vienna 118; and in Rome 243!! So that in this case also Protestant London is the best, and Rome the seat of the Pope is the worst. According to this, London is more than sixty times better than Rome. Could a more damaging record of Romanism be offered to the world than this? We here see that where Popery is strongest, there crime is greatest. That where the Pope holds his seat and where he has everything his own way; where he reigns both as a civil and spiritual ruler, where every branch of the government is under his control, there crime and licentiousness most abound. On the other hand, where Protestantism is strongest, where she is permitted to control and direct her forces, there crime is less and virtue most conspicuous. Who does not know that a large percentage of the criminals that fill our prisons and penitentiaries are Roman Catholics?

The New York *Tribune*, published last August a carefully prepared table for that city, placing this matter in its proper light:

"While due proportion of arrests to nationality required 567 in every 1,000 native born, there were but 308: a very large share of which were certainly, though natives, yet the children of Irish papists, where the Irish should have had but 222, they really had 506. The German proportion was 147, but they had only 104; all others, chiefly foreigners, required 63, and had 81. The native arrests were 308 in 1,000: all foreign together were 692 in 1,000. Native arrests were only fifty-three per cent. of due proportion; Irish arrests were 129 per cent. more than their share. The Germans are considerably under their share, and other foreigners are a little over. Now, when we consider that three-fourths of the arrests classed as natives are the children of foreign parents, and substantially foreign themselves, we have in round numbers of arrests about as follows, for the ten years: United States, 55,000; Ireland, 460,000; Germany, 115,000; all others, 86,000. Such is the lesson of the police records."

The same significant lesson, so damaging to the character of Romanism, is taught in the results of the recent election in Bavaria, where

Influence of Popery. 37

the Roman Church is strongly in the ascendant. The clergy there have entire charge of the schools, and demanded the defeat of the Liberal party as the only safeguard of the morals and religion of the country. Since the election a Liberal member of Parliament has prepared a chart, showing that those portions where the extreme church party gained their most decided victories, were those where there were the greatest number of crimes and dishonorable punishments. In lower Bavaria, which sent none but priests and ultramontanes to the house, he found that for every 100,000 inhabitants there were during the year, 29 crimes and 137 years of imprisonment, while in the most Liberal provinces there were but $6\frac{1}{2}$ crimes and about 31 years imprisonment. This chart gives ocular proof that in this Papal country, the supremacy of the clergy has tended to the ignorance and vice of the people.

Now can any one imagine that the interests of our country, its free institutions, the general intelligence of its people, its progressive development and prosperity, etc., would be safe for an hour in the hands of those who have such a record? Who are furnishing mobs, filling our prisons, and supplying nearly every victim for the gallows? And who boasts of the unchangeable character of their system—its oneness in all countries and in all ages? No one can doubt what she has done in Bavaria, in Belgium, in Austria, in Spain, in Portugal, and in the South American Republics, she would do in this country if she had the power. Even France, under her sway, although boasting of the most glittering artistic civilization in the world, has thirty-three per cent. of her population that can neither read or write. The Sabbath is but little else than a grand holiday for amusement and recreation.

Disguise it as we may, if ever the time come when the government of these United States passes into the hands of the Roman Catholics, our doom as a free and prosperous people will be sealed. Our pleasant places will become frightful wastes; and an intellectual and moral darkness, ten-fold more hideous than nature's solitude, will spread throughout this land; and our free institutions, endeared to us by the blood of our fathers, and a thousand hallowed recollections of the past, shoved from their moorings will sink in an ocean of storm.

CHAPTER III.
Romish Aggression.

That Romanism has been for a long time bending all her energies to secure a controlling political influence in these United States, no one can doubt who has paid the least attention to the history of the past. Crippled seriously in the old world by the Reformation, which broke the mighty spell of her power that held all Europe in ecclesiastical slavery, she has turned her attention to our hitherto prosperous Protestant country, as an inviting field for the establishment of her hateful supremacy. She has, under cover of religious toleration, steadily pursued an aggressive policy that has been unnoted, save by a few who have generally been regarded as alarmists, (and consequently unheeded in their warnings,) until now she boldly advances to assume menacing attitudes of hostility to our free institutions, loudly boasting of her present and prospective conquests.

Our Fathers laid the foundation of our free institutions on the bases of a distinct recognition of the Bible and the right of the masses to a personal knowledge of its sublime truths. Its teachings of morality are interwoven in our institutions, and incorporated in our laws and customs. This distinct recognition of the Bible, and the right of all to a knowledge of its contents—whether found in the Constitution or on the statute book, or in the laws regulating judicial proceedings, or in the enforced observance of the Sabbath, or wherever found, prove beyond a doubt that they intended this land to be a Bible land. This important fact has been clearly set forth by a Roman Catholic, in a recent letter to a New York secular paper, in which he protests against reading the Bible in the public schools on this very account. He says : " The Bible is the chief and sole source of Protestant beliefs : it is the potent weapon of the Protestant power. The most powerful engine of Protestantism is the Bible. The Bible, the whole Bible, and nothing but the Bible, is the slogan and watchword of the Protestant chieftains. In this Bible is the foundation, the superstructure, the inside and outside, the length, width, height, and depth of the Protestant system." We accept this declaration as strictly true. The Bible has been made the bases of all that we as Protestants hold dear. Our free institutions owe their existence to the Bible. The Roman Catholics however, who are mostly foreigners, and who have sworn eternal allegiance to a foreign despot, propose to overturn and break down these institutions as transmitted to us by our Fathers, by striking at their very foundation—the Bible. This hierarchy that for three hundred years, by wars and persecution, sought to take the Bible from the Waldenses, true to their instincts, have now commenced hostilities against the Bible in our very midst. They aim a blow at our national life, by striking at a vital element of our sixty-five thousand public schools, in demanding the expulsion of the Bible therefrom.

But this is not all. They evidently intend to secure the utter destruction of the entire school system itself. Many of the Roman Catholic journals and priests make no effort to conceal such a design. The Bible is made the specious pretext for a formidable combination against the whole system of popular education. This is the legitimate result of the spirit of Popery. In its very nature there is an ever-living spirit of antagonism to all of our free institutions. Let us not shut our eyes to the fact that Romanism is now struggling for power which is already felt in the legislation of our country and in our courts, and is even now enlisting in its interests some of the leading politicians of the day, and is manipulating and controlling to a great extent a great political party. They are outstripping every single Protestant denomination in the country, in the erection of costly churches in the most eligible localities; they are rapidly filling the land with monasteries, nunneries and sectarian schools. They are bending all their energies to secure official positions of profit and power throughout the nation. In many of our principal cities, most of the offices are already in the hands of Romanists, where they by their energy and unification actually control the political primary meetings and the elections. This influence is rapidly extending to the States, and will not stop short of the general government, unless met by timely resistance. Already many of the leading Generals of the army and commanders in the navy are Romanists. They are aspiring every where to positions of influence and power. The city of New York to-day is absolutely governed by an Irish-Roman-Catholic constituency, which will not permit any one who is not a papist, or who will not become pledged to stand by and promote the interest of Popery, to hold any office whatever in the Corporation. Hence a majority of all the city officers are Irish Catholics. The exact number I am not able to name. The Tract Society Almanac for 1870 contains the following statistics in reference to this subject: "They (Romanists) have the Sheriff, Comptroller, Chamberlain, President, and fourteen of nineteen Councilmen; the Clerk, and eight of ten Supervisors, five Justices of the Courts of Records, all the civil justices, two Congressmen, three of the five State Senators, and eighteen of twenty-one Assemblymen."

Aggression of Popery.

As they have been for some time steadily increasing in this respect, it is but fair to infer that the proportion of Roman Catholic office-holders has increased during the past year, so that now they must have well nigh all the offices in their own hands.

About in keeping with the above astounding facts, are the large appropriations secured by them from the city government and the State legislature to build up their peculiar sectarian interests, to the great detriment of the public school system.

We ask attention to the following table of moneys voted from the public treasury of the city of New York for the past ten years. The aggregates are made from details carefully gathered from official documents by the editor of the *Christian World*.

A. D.	Roman Catholic Institutions.	All other Religious and Charitable Institutions: Protestant, Jewish and Public.	TOTALS.
1860		5,430 00	5,430 00
1861	18,791 27	12,769 53	31,560 80
1862	9,153 63	36,099 86	45,253 49
1863	78,000 00	13,522 11	91,522 11
1864	73,000 00	14,094 40	87,094 40
1865	40,000 00	23,552 66	63,552 66
1866	21,607 24	25,799 78	47,407 02
1867	120,000 00	13,100 40	133,100 40
1868	124,424 60	28,872 38	153,296 98
1869	412,062 26	116,680 21	528,742 47
Ten Yrs.	$897,039 00	$289,921 33	$1,186,960 00

Upon the last of these items, published in detail by the Union League, we add the comment of two journals. The *Independent*, under the heading of "Sectarian Robberies," makes this earnest appeal:—

"Read the report from the Union League Club, on the robbery of the public treasury by the Roman Catholic politicians and their allies. We give up two or three columns to it; and we would devote the whole fifty-six to the subject, if the people of this city and this State, and the whole country, could thereby be roused to the duty of the hour. Again and again we have called public attention to the inroads which Romanism is making upon the public money,—applying the Taxes of the people to Sectarian purposes,—until, to all intents and purposes, the Roman Catholic is to-day the Established Religion of New York. Its schools and its churches, its priests and its nuns, are in large part supported by the money of Protestants, extorted by oppressive taxation, and paid over to the treasury of the Romish Church.

"Citizens of New York! Protestant Christians of the United States! we ask you to ponder upon the statements made in this report. It comes, indeed, from a political club; but if there is one statement there made which can be challenged and confuted, let it be done. It is time to meet the question where the Romanists have put it, and the people must come to the rescue, or the Romanist's Church will soon have the State and the country under its iron heel."

The *Presbyterian Banner* suggests two reflections:—

"One is, that the servility of American citizens who will tolerate this gross injustice is more amazing than the arrogance which has demanded for one sect this colossal bribe. That ecclesiastics have a proclivity to handle the funds of other people, is attested by the whole history of the Romish Church; but that free-born Americans should cringe before the haughty prelates of that sect, is humiliating in the extreme.

"Another reflection is, that the danger which seems to attend the handling of Protestant Bibles does not attach itself to Protestant dollars. The hands which would tear, with pious horror, from the walls of our schoolrooms, the ten commandments, especially the eighth, as printed from the Protestant Bible, lovingly unclasp to receive, in great part from Protestant tax-payers, the generous tribute of more than four hundred thousand dollars in a single city for a single year."

Surely here is enough to make every Protestant and every lover of our Free Institutions ashamed of the public apathy that has made these appropriations possible. These astounding developments are enough to make our very ears tingle.

The *American Messenger*, in speaking of the above, says:—

"The report further states that in 1866 the city government gave to the archbishop of the favored sect half a block of ground in Madison Avenue, now worth $200,000, for one dollar a year. In 1852 they gave to the same sect the fee of a whole block of ground in Fifth avenue, worth $1,500,000, for $83.32, and in 1864 paid them $24,000 for the privilege of extending Madison Avenue across it, and $8,929 to pay the assessments for opening it. They have also given the next block to them, worth the same amount, for one dollar a year, thus giving $3,200,000 worth of real estate to a single sect for sectarian purposes."

It would be difficult to conceive of a greater scandal to religion than the course that has been pursued in New York by reckless political demagogues in catering to the wishes of Popery, to secure their votes for party triumph. Politicians in many instances have not scrupled to sacrifice the public interest to sectarian cupidity to secure political power.

Their aggressive operations, however, are not confined to New York. They are busily engaged in carrying out their opposing policy wherever there is the least possible chance of success. They secured the expulsion of the Bible from the public schools of Cincinnati, and interdicted the singing of hymns, or opening the exercises with prayer, until their treasonable action was set aside by the Supreme Court. They have secured, I am told, the incorporation of their own sectarian schools as public schools in the city of New Haven, to be supported at the public expense. They have also had the audacity to insist upon the introduction of their catechism into the public schools of San Francisco.

The plain and common sense view of all this is, that they intend to make Romanism the State Religion of this country, to be supported by direct taxes levied on Protestants as well as others throughout the land, as has been their practice in all countries where they have had the power. Rome means to be dominant in these United States at whatever cost.

Encouraged partly by her success in the past, and partly by the indifference of some, and the connivance of others, she has ventured to unmask her batteries and open her fire upon the very encampment of Protestantism. As the Bible has ever been the bulwark of our free institutions, and the foundation of our faith, it becomes the principal object of her attack. Her whole past history is replete with evidence of her opposition to the circulation of the Scriptures among the masses. From the first establishment of the American Bible Society, its chief and most persistent opponent has been the Church of Rome. It is not, therefore, at all strange that they should desire, or even seek to banish the inspired volume from our public schools. But who could have believed that within so short a time, they could have secured such an influence in political circles at some of our leading centres, as to either expel the Bible from our public schools or secure the passage of such laws as shall tax even majorities to uphold institutions which they abhor, and which are known to be antagonistic to our free institutions, and that the moneyed resources of the

State should, through their manipulations, be handed over to the Romish hierarchy by godless politicians for the maintenance of Popery in our midst? Who could have believed that the arrogance of Romanism in these United States would so soon be developed in such an open and defiant attack as has already been made? The animus of all this is not difficult to understand. Their persistent attacks upon the entire educational interests of the various States all look to one great focal purpose. The Romish hierarchy most intensely hate the liberal education afforded to the masses by our public school system. Hence the Jesuitical effort is most adroitly made to break them down. There can be no reasonable doubt that this is the object. The expulsion of the Bible is only one step in that direction. When this is accomplished, other demands will undoubtedly be made. The same spirit will next demand that all school books that refer to the Bible—to its authority, its inspiration, its doctrines, its moral precepts, and its teaching—be also expelled from these institutions. There will be the same reason for this, as there is for the other. Where would be the consistency of yielding the one and not the others? What would be the character of our schools, should the imperious demands of Rome be obeyed until every book impregnated with the literature of the Bible, or that should teach the precepts of Christ, or refer to the Divine government, or the providences of God as taught in his word, should be expurgated? Who does not see that this would be the destruction of our entire school system? It therefore becomes us to meet this question at the very threshold of Roman aggression. We had as well meet it first as last. It is impossible to avoid it. The crisis is upon us. To yield to the expulsion of the Bible will only be to remove the conflict to another quarter.

CHAPTER IV.

The avowed Purposes of Rome in the United States.

ONE of the leading objects of Rome has been, in all ages, to obtain control of governments and subjugate the nations of the earth to her iron sceptre. Her theory has been, and still is, that Christ gave to Peter two swords—one the symbol of spiritual authority, the other of political rule. And as all the authority of St. Peter is invested in the Pope, as his lineal descendant and rightful representative, it is claimed that he not only has the right to govern the world, but is in duty bound, to the extent of his ability, through his 8,584 Jesuits and almost innumerable number of priests, bishops, and archbishops, by skill or force, by fair means or foul, to get possession of every sceptre, of every legislature, and every department of political power.

That they are bending all their energies to get political control of this country, can not be doubted by any one who has given the subject any very thoughtful consideration. The whole hierarchy in this country is working with a most determined will for this purpose, and not without encouragement of ultimate success.

The danger that threatens us is one of no ordinary magnitude. It is nothing less than the overthrow and destruction of our free institutions. Romanism is incompatible with Protestantism. The Roman Catholic Church claims that when she is placed on an equality before the law with other religious sects, she is deprived of her just rights, as she does not admit that other sects should be tolerated at all. She has accepted the advantages that Protestant toleration has given her in this country, only so long as she is powerless to control the destinies of the nation. When that point is reached, she intends to revolutionize our institutions. These declarations are not based merely upon her known hostility to Republican institutions generally, but upon her repeated avowals, as proclaimed in her accredited journals, and by some of her leading divines, of a fixed purpose to labor for this very thing. For this purpose they propose to get control, first of the political machinery of the States, and then of the National Government.

The *Catholic World*, in a leading article of July, entitled "The Catholics of the Nineteenth Century," says:

"To the Catholic of to-day is committed the obligation and business of perpetuating and *regenerating society*, purifying legislation, enforcing the administration of the laws, and setting an example of private and public virtue, justice, moderation, and forbearance, he has been furnished with an omnipotent weapon with which to accomplish this great work, and he is provided with an unerring guide to direct him in the administration of these important trusts. We do not hesitate to affirm that in performing our duties as citizens, electors, and public officers, we should *always, and under all circumstances, act simply as Catholics;* that we should be governed and directed by the immutable principles of our religion, and should take dogmatic faith and the conclusions drawn from it, as expressed and defined in Catholic philosophy, theology, and morality, as the only rule of our private, public, and political conduct."

In the above extract two things are boldly and distinctly stated, namely, the work to be done, and the manner in which it is to be accomplished. They propose to "regenerate society" in the interest of Romanism, in the most objectionable sense of the term. That this is what is meant is evident from the manner in which they propose to work out this change in society. "The unerring guide to direct him" in this work, is none other than the Pope of Rome; under whose guidance they are to simply act, not as politicians for the good or success of the party or its principles, but as "*Catholics.*"

Again says the same paper:

"*A land of promise*, a land flowing with milk and honey, *is spread out before them (the Catholics), and*

Avowed Purposes of Rome. 53

offered for their acceptance. The means placed at their disposal for securing this rich possession are not the sword, or wars of extermination waged against the enemies of their religion, but, instead, *the mild and peaceful influence of the ballot, directed by instructed Catholic conscience and enlightened Catholic intelligence.*"

We are not told in the above who has offered this country to the Catholics. But we doubt not that there are plenty of politicians reckless enough, and godless enough, to sell the cause of freedom and their country, for Catholic votes. At all events, it is distinctly affirmed they intend to secure the control of this country through the ballot-box. The same paper adds :

"It is in the power of the Catholic voter of the nineteenth century to achieve a consummation such as perhaps saints and prophets have dreamed, but never seen."

Some of the beauties of this consummation so ardently desired, are pointed out in the following extract:

"She (the Church) speaks always and everywhere with the authority of God, as the final cause of creation, and therefore her words are law, her commands are the commands of God. This being so, it is clear that *religious liberty must consist in the unrestrained freedom and independence of the church* to teach and *govern all men and nations, princes and people, rulers and ruled,* in all things enjoined by the teleological law of man's existence, and therefore in the recognition and maintenance for the church of that very supreme authority *which the popes have always claimed*, and against which the Reformation protested, and which secular princes are generally disposed to resist when it crosses their pride, their policy, their ambition, or their love of power."

The idea of "religious liberty" with Romanists has always been that of liberty for the Church to "govern all men and nations, princes and people," according to her own pleasure. This theory, which she carried out in former times by dethroning kings, absolving subjects from their oaths of allegiance to lawful rulers, laying whole countries under an interdict, and burning thousands of those who refused to bow to her authority, she still maintains, and proposes to make it supreme in these United States.

"Heresy and infidelity have not, and never had, and never can have any right, being as they undeniably are, contrary to the law of God."—*Brownson's Quarterly, January*, 1852.

"Heresy and unbelief are crimes; and in Christian countries, as in Italy and Spain, for instance, where the Catholic religion is the essential law of the land; they are punished as other crimes."—*Archbishop Kendrick.*

No language could more distinctly declare that Romanism is the same to-day, that it was during the horrors of the Inquisition. They only then declared that Protestantism was heresy, and deserved to be punished as other great crimes; and having the power, carried their conviction into execution. Besides, in the above extract the bishop grossly insults the people of the United States by his malicious insinuation that this is not a Christian nation. If the above, however, is not sufficient to satisfy the most sceptical that Rome will persecute Protestants whenever, and wherever she has the power, then let him ponder the following:

"Religious liberty is merely endured until the opposite can be carried into operation without peril to the Catholic world."—*Bishop O'Connor of Pittsburgh.*

So "*Religious liberty is merely endured until the opposite can be carried,*" or in other words, Protestantism is merely endured until Romanism has secured the necessary power to suppress every other form of religion, if needs be, by kindling anew the fires of persecution. Who can doubt after reading the above that Rome is the same in spirit and nature to-day as she was when she made the blood of Protestants to flow like water on every side by her cruel and inhuman policy of utter extermination? Perfectly in keeping with the above is the following from high and unquestionable authority:

"If the Catholics ever gain, which they surely will, an immense numerical majority, religious freedom in this country will be at an end!"—*Archbishop of St. Louis.*

Could any form of words be more explicit than this? Can any one fail to understand the determined policy of Romanism in these United States? In the last quotation, two things are most emphatically and distinctly affirmed, namely, that Catholics will ultimately gain "an immense numerical majority," and in the next place, when this is gained, "religious freedom in this country will be at an end." And all this from one of their own Archbishops of the present day and in our very midst.

While no intelligent person can well shut his eyes to the intolerant and despotic character of Rome as naturally and essentially antagonistic to our free institutions, yet few, comparatively speaking, seem to have waked up to the fact that she has already entered upon a grand crusade for the subversion of our liberties; that she has even now an organized system for the speedy accomplishment of this object; that an actual purpose to this end pervades every department of her government, permeating every one of her religious orders, as a controlling influence; and that she is bending all her energies to the acquisition of religious, social and political predominance in our midst as an important part of this grand scheme.

That there are numerous difficulties in the way of the consummation of this undertaking, no one can doubt; but, then, let it be remembered she has already gained immense advantages in spite of these difficulties. If these successes, and her astounding declarations, fail to awaken public attention to the greatness of our danger; if the great mass of Protestants can be persuaded that there is no very great cause of alarm after all; if they can only be induced to keep quiet, to sleep on, to do nothing, the road will be open, and when their power is once established in these United States, our sun will have set.

CHAPTER V.

Further Cause for Alarm from Popery.

THERE are various other causes in connection with what has already been stated, that may well excite the apprehensions of Protestants for the safety of our free institutions. One of these is the rapid growth of Romanism in this country. While in Europe, where it is best known by sad experience, it is steadily loosing its hold upon the popular mind, and while even its own communicants, in many instances in that country, are in open rebellion against its arrogant assumptions; here, it is steadily increasing in numbers, in influence, in wealth, and in power; while it is petted, and favored, and caressed, even by government officials, more than all other denominations together.

As to the amount of the yearly increase of papists, or its per centage, or the relation it bears to the increase of our entire population, it is not easy to determine. This is owing to the want of full and complete statistics of the number of their priests, churches, communicants, colleges, schools, monasteries, convents, etc. To secure accuracy it would be necessary to have, not only complete statistics for the present, but that they extend back through a number of years. But Roman Catholic publications are very deficient in such information.

Dr. Mattison furnishes a table in his work on Romanism*, from the *Catholic World*, which is as follows :

	Catholics.	Whole Population.	Proportion.
In 1808	100,000	6,000,000	1–65th.
" 1830	450,000	13,000,000	1–29th.
" 1840	960,000	17,000,000	1–18th.
" 1850	2,150,000	23,000,000	1–11th.
" 1860	4,400,000	31,000,000	1–7th.
" 1870	7,000,000	39,000,000	1–5th.†

In Appleton's Cyclopediæ for 1864, article *Roman Catholic Church*, it is stated that, "The increase between 1840 and 1860, was 125 upon each hundred, while the nation only increased by 36 to a hundred; between 1850 and 1860 the increase was 109 upon a hundred, while the nation increased only 30 upon a hundred. Should things go on only as they have hitherto done, the Catholic population will be one-fifth of the whole in 1870, and nearly one-third in 1900."

Now, whether the above be strictly true or not, it is patent to all that Romanists are rapidly increasing on every side. It is stated in their Family Almanac for 1871, that in 1816

---

* Page 64.   † This line I have changed to make it correspond with the present time.

there were in all New England, only two thousand Catholics, with two priests and a bishop, while now there are nearly one million in the same territory.

An article appeared in the American Messenger not long since, headed "*A great increase,*" in which it was stated that "there are now 100 churches and 200,000 Roman Catholics in Rhode Island and Connecticut, where fifty years ago there were but three families of Romanists."

What is true of the New England States in this respect is true, in a great measure, of all the States. It is supposed that there are some 400,000 in the city of New York alone, and they claim over 800,000 in the State.

This rapid growth of Romanism in the United States is not so much to be wondered at, however, when we take into consideration the fact that it is estimated that between one and two hundred thousand are added to her communion yearly by emigration alone. This enables her to move with rapid strides toward the establishment of her supremacy; to outstrip any other denomination in the erection of costly and imposing structures for church purposes. Says Dr. Mattison, after presenting several valuable statistical tables: "It would appear that the Roman Catholics have expended about four times as much money in building churches since 1860, as the Methodist Episcopal Church has."*

And again : "Though the number of their priests is small compared with the number of Protestant ministers, yet they are sufficient to man all their churches, and are rapidly increasing. And what is *more alarming*, many of them are American born."

It does not, however, lessen the cause for alarm to know that the increase of Papists in the United States is principally in consequence of emigration. European Papists are certainly no better than American converts to Romanism. From whatever cause her increase among us proceeds, we have the same reason to apprehend the subversion of our liberties whenever she secures the necessary strength.

Says the Tablet : " Catholics are increasing rapidly in the United States, and it is to be *expected that they will introduce and observe Catholic usages, and these all the world knows differ from those of Puritans.*" Of course they do. This is frank.

A writer in one of the Western "*Advocates,*" says : "The Papists are rapidly conquering the great West. Their agency is the school. The property of the Roman Catholics in the new city of Leavenworth, Kansas, is, from the published estimates, some $475,000, while all other

* Page 42.

Christian denominations in the same city, including our own, is less than $100,000. Sustained by all this wealth, the agency of the Romish Church is their schools for girls. Such a school is established in every large town, and these schools are chiefly supplied with scholars by the patronage of Protestants."

Much of their success is undoubtedly to be attributed to their sectarian schools, which for some reason or other have unfairly got the reputation of being superior to Protestant schools, in consequence of which they secure the attendance of many Protestant children who ultimately become Romanists. These schools are proselyting agencies. Hence, while thousands of their own children are growing up in ignorance, unable to read or write, Protestant girls are offered tuition on very low terms, in order to instil into their minds the principles of Popery.

To suppose their schools superior in any sense to Protestant schools, is to betray an utter want of information of their character. Protestant schools, so far as teaching and thoroughness of education are concerned, are vastly superior to Roman Catholic schools. This is even admitted by Romanists themselves. O. A. Brownson, a rigid Roman Catholic, a leading writer, and thoroughly acquainted with all Catholic institutions of learning in this country, says:

Danger from Popery. 63

"They (Catholic schools) *practically fail to recognise human progress*, and thus fail to recognise the continuance and successive evolution of the idea in the life of humanity. *** They *do not educate their pupils to be at home and at their ease in their own age and country, or train them to be living, thinking, and energetic men, prepared for the work which actually awaits them either in Church or State.* As far as we are able to trace the effect of the most approved Catholic education of our day, whether at home or abroad, it tends *to repress* rather than quicken the life of the pupil, *to unfit* rather than prepare him for the active and zealous discharge either of his religious or his social duties. They who are educated in *our schools seem misplaced and mistimed in the world, as if born and educated for a world that has ceased to exist.* *** Comparatively *few* of them (Catholic graduates) take their stand as *scholars* or as men, on a level with the Catholics of non-Catholic colleges, and those who do take that stand do it by *throwing aside nearly all they learned from their Alma Mater*, and adopting the ideas and principles, the modes of thought and action they find in the general civilization of the country in which they live. *** The cause of the failure of what we call Catholic education is, in our judgment, in the fact that we educate *not for the present*, or the future, but for the *past*. *** We do not mean that the dogmas are not scrupulously taught in all our schools and colleges, nor that the words of the Catechism are not duly insisted upon. We concede this, and that gives to our so-called Catholic schools a merit which no others have or can have. It is now behind the times, and *unfits* rather than prepares the student for taking an active part in the work of his own day and generation. There can be no question that what passes for Catholic education in *this or any other country*, has its ideal of perfection in the *past*, and that it *resists* as un-Catholic, irreligious and opposed to God, *the tendencies of modern civilization.* *** The work it gives its subjects or prepares them to perform is not the work of carrying it forward, but that of *resisting it, driving it back*, anathematizing it as at war with the Gospel, and either of neglecting it altogether and taking refuge in the cloister, in an exclusive or exaggerated asceticism, always bordering on immorality, or of restoring a former order of civilization, no longer a living order, and which humanity has evidently left behind, and is resolved shall never be restored."*

It would be well for all Protestants who may contemplate sending their children to Catholic institutions, under the impression that they are better than our own schools, to carefully ponder the foregoing statements made by one of their own honored writers, who was eminently qualified to judge of their true merit, and who can never be charged with being prejudiced against Catholic institutions of any kind. These are the kind of schools that we are asked to support by appropriating a portion of the school fund of the State; mere sectarian schools. And yet, as strange as it may appear, a large number of Protestant girls are found in their schools, receiving instruction in the peculiarities of their sectarianism. Of these it is estimated that on an average *seven* out of every *ten* become Papists.

A lady educated in a nunnery at Montreal,

* January No. of Brownson's Review for 1862.

states, that of forty girls from Protestant families in the United States, who were there when she was there, all but herself and one other became Roman Catholics. Another lady who had been educated in a convent, says, as reported by Dr. Mattison: "Warn the people wherever you go, of the danger of sending their children to Roman Catholic schools. They are the poorest schools in the country for real education, and are the chief agency of Romanism to seduce the children of reputable families into the Roman Church. I have passed through the terrible ordeal, and know what it is." Says Dr. Mattison: "They have no more successful agency at work in this country than their various female academies; and all Protestant parents, who do not wish their children ruined, should keep them from Roman Catholic schools as they would keep them from the gates of death."

To these sectarian schools, and the large emigration that is yearly pouring in upon our shores, are we to look for the vast accumulation of the numbers of Romanists in our land; and, especially, is the increase so large from the latter, that notwithstanding the annual loss to the Romish Church of thousands of her communicants from the old world, there are still enough left, that remain true to her interests, as to render her power and influence more formidable every succeeding year. In this way, the governments of our large cities, which are centers of a potential political influence, are, one after another, falling into the hands of the Papists, to be controlled by them for the advancement of their own power.

The influence of Rome in our large cities is already alarming, and fearfully on the increase. In most cases she holds the balance of power so as to secure important concessions from godless politicians. These concentric circles of Papal influence spreading from each of these centers will ere long meet and overlap each other throughout our land.

Another circumstance that adds materially to the influence and power of Romanism, is the compactness of her system. This is owing to the perfect and complete centralization of her forces. The Romish priests and bishops, the emissaries of the Pope, are thoroughly unified and determined in their efforts to extend and perpetuate the power of their church in our midst, to which they have sworn allegiance. Let it be remembered that their priests and bishops are nearly all foreigners, in the service of a foreign power. That they have been schooled in foreign seminaries, in the doctrine of passive obedience; that while they are not bound by any of the ordinary ties to our government and country, they are bound by pecuniary interest, by their love of promotion, as well as by the most sacred pledges and solemn oaths of consecration, to serve to the best of their ability a foreign despot; that they, to all intents and purposes, constitute the Roman Catholic Church in the United States, the laity having no voice; moreover, the American bishops not being chosen by their clergy or cathedral chapters, as they are in some countries, but being appointed at the mere pleasure of the Pope, are among the most zealous supporters of the extreme ultramontane principles of Popery. This zealous devotion of the American bishops to Roman intolerance and despotism, has been so decided and outspoken as to have recently called forth an expression of surprise from the liberal press of Germany. We venture to say that the influence of the Court of Rome over the Episcopal body in this country is stronger than it is over the bishops of any other part of the world. This hierarchy, which is a sort of politico-ecclesiastical organization, controlled by a foreign despot, and banded together, and bound by oaths and obligations such as are unknown to any other denomination, controls and directs the laity absolutely according to its own will.

This is what gives them their immense power. This constitutes the secret of their success. While Protestants are split up into various organizations, and are divided in their political views, and consequently in their action, the Romanists are a unit, and are moving on under their leaders with the precision of trained battalions to the subversion of our liberties. Just as ten thousand men properly drilled, equipped and officered, would be more than a match for a hundred thousand that were wanting in all these things, so the Roman Catholics, notwithstanding the smallness of their number when compared to Protestants, yet through their superior drill and union of efforts are securing victory after victory. If Protestants should fail to wake up to the danger that threatens to overwhelm them, it is not difficult to foretell the end.

Another source of evil and cause of alarm is the fraternity of Jesuits, who at this very time are swarming in our land. They, as we have seen, are the *sworn enemies* of our free institutions. This society, which has been notorious throughout the world for its infamy, and which has been expelled for political intrigue from almost every government in Europe, more than thirty times—a fact unparalleled in the history of the wickedest combination ever formed beside—against which, in former times, such a storm of indignation arose on every side, that Pope Clement IX. in a bull suppressed the order altogether in these words, *" So that the name of the company shall be, and is, forever extinguish-*

ed and suppressed." Yet this hateful Order was, in spite of Roman infallibility, restored by a counter bull of Pope Pius VII., and now is the right arm of the Papacy in this country.

And now the great question that looms up before us in the moral horizon is, shall we yield this glorious country of ours, our free institutions purchased by the blood of our forefathers, our religious liberties planted amid suffering by our noble sires, and all that we as Protestants hold dear, shall we give up all these without a struggle? Shall we not rather forget our differences, and unite our forces to oppose, and if possible to roll back this foreign aggression, this tide of spiritual despotism, that threatens to overwhelm us? We admire a hopeful spirit, and deprecate despondency and every false alarm; but there are times when to cry peace and safety, is the rankest treason, is certain suicide. Such a time we believe has now arrived; that the Philistines are already upon us; that our religious liberties are at stake. This is not mere fancy. That to save our Protestant institutions will involve a mighty struggle, a terrible conflict, is no longer a conjecture, or a probability, but to many minds, an absolute certainty.

CHAPTER VI.

Romanists versus Public Schools.

THE dogmatical, intolerant, and anti-Scriptural spirit of Popery, that has all through the past sought to subject to its absolute power and control, the entire human race, soul and body, for time and eternity, in order to build up an odious despotism; and which has arrayed her against the Bible, against free institutions, against liberty of conscience, against the spirit of scientific progress, and against all the live forces and tendencies of the present age, has very naturally arrayed her against our public school system in these United States. In this attempt of Rome to break down and overthrow our educational institutions, she is but acting in accordance with her long settled policy of subjecting every thing to herself. Our public schools have never pleased the Romish hierarchs, and never can. Modify them as we may, they will be offensive to them, so long as they cannot use them in their own interest. This fact may as well be understood first as last.

"We hold education to be a function of the Church, not of the State; and in our case, we do not, and we *will not*, accept the State as educator."—*Tablet, Dec.* 25.

On a recent trial in Ireland, a priest testified that he had positive orders from Archbishop MacHale to refuse all the sacraments, even at the hour of death, to those who send their children to the free schools. The same spirit is now manifesting itself in our midst against our own schools, not against their present form, but against the entire system. The expressed willingness of many Protestants to banish the Bible from our public schools, in order to conciliate Romanists, while it accomplishes nothing, is far more complimentary to their hearts than to their heads. Nor has the proposition of others to introduce the Roman Catholic translation of the Scriptures into our common schools, met with any better success in diminishing their hostility to our educational system.

"We tell our respected contemporary, therefore, that if the Catholic translation of the Book of Holy Writ * * * were to be dissected by the ablest Catholic theologian in the land, and merely lessons to be taken from it—with all the notes and comments, in the popular edition, and others added, with the highest Catholic endorsement—and if these admirable Bible lessons, and these alone, were to be ruled as to be read in all the public schools, this would not diminish, in any substantial degree, the objections we Catholics have to letting Catholic children attend the public schools. *"* *There is no possible programme of common school instruction that the Catholic Church can permit her children to accept.*"—*Freeman's Journal*, Nov. 20.

Is not the above language sufficiently explicit and decided to satisfy even the most sceptical, that our public schools have in the Roman Catholics a most determined and implacable foe?

If any, however, are so incredulous as to still doubt the designs of the Romish Church to destroy our public school system, so vital to these institutions and the welfare of coming generations—if any still believe the above astounding declarations to be local and exceptional, let them cast their eyes abroad to other lands for an evidence of her character and policy. Look at their recent attempts to overthrow the public schools of Holland. They were not only accorded the full enjoyment of political rights, by that Protestant country after they had drenched the soil with Protestant blood, by the horrors of a most terrible persecution; but in 1853, they were granted the privilege of establishing five dioceses. In 1857, Holland introduced our public school system of popular education. For years there was no complaint. Protestant and Catholic children sat together in the same seats. At length, however, the viper which they had warmed into life, and which they had nursed and clothed with important privileges, began to show its fangs. The schools were by them denounced. The Roman Bishops in 1868, anathematized them, and ordered their people to abandon them and

Romanists versus Public Schools. 73

erect their own schools, or if too poor to do so, to leave their children uneducated. The Roman Catholics brought to bear all of their powerful agencies to break up the public school system. The people were aroused. The most intense feeling was excited by this bigoted interference upon the part of Papists. The people rallied at the following election, and decided by a large majority to continue the public school system.

Popery is the determined foe of public schools every where. There is no possibility of disguising this fact, or longer shutting our eyes to the crisis that is upon us. To yield one iota to the unreasonable demands of Rome, in reference to the school question, is to give up a great principle, is to surrender an outpost of Protestantism, a battery, that is sure to be turned against us. Let it be distinctly understood by all, that Popery seeks not the modification of our public schools, but their utter destruction. Rome will be satisfied with nothing short of this. She intensely hates every thing that is Protestant, or of Protestant origin. Every thing that is essential to Protestant principles, or Protestant institutions, is under her curse, and must be put down to the extent of her power.

The speciousness of the plea of Romanists, for their share of the school funds to educate their children in their own way, should deceive no one. However plausible in appearance, it is destructive in its aim. Every one must see, that to give to Romanists their proportion of the school fund, must be destructive of the whole system. In the rural districts, it is often difficult and costly at best to maintain a sufficient number of schools, so as to have them near enough to all the children to secure their attendance. To give a part of the funds to Romanists would be to so divide, and weaken thousands of districts, as to render it impossible to support common schools at all. But this is not the whole of the difficulty by any means. If we give to Roman Catholics their share of the school fund, as they are now demanding, for sectarian purposes, we submit to be taxed to support a particular church. Here we would then have the very worst features of a church establishment, in which one man would be taxed to teach and support the religion of another man, in direct violation of the Constitution, and the principles upon which our free institutions are established. This would be substantially the endowment of a sect. The money would be of course used for sectarian purposes; to build up a system of antagonism to our free institutions. Nor is this the whole of the difficulty that would legitimately grow out of such an appropriation. If we give to the Roman Catholics a part of the school fund for sectarian purposes, we would be under the same obligation to give to every other sect that might demand it, their proportion also. Methodists, Baptists, Presbyterians, Congregationalists, Episcopalians, and every other religious order would have just as valid a claim for their proportion of the school fund as would Romanists. Even Jews and Infidels might make their respective demands with equal propriety. Nor would it be likely to end here. Some are already demanding that there shall be separate schools for colored children. Next, perhaps, the Germans may demand German schools, the Chinese separate schools, and so on, until our schools would be so divided and subdivided into sectarian and race schools, that there would not be a vestige left of our present public school system.

Such a course would inevitably lead to endless strife and competition among the sects in the legislative halls. Bickerings, jealousies, and incurable animosities would be engendered. The necessary divisions and subdivisions, and consequent multiplied buildings and teachers, would, to say the least, involve an immense waste of funds. At the same time it would fail, to a great extent, to furnish education to a large portion of our population which belong to no sect. Such a sectarian system of State education could never be maintained.

Now, who can be so blind as not to see that

this clamor of Romanists for a share of the school fund, for sectarian purposes, is the entering wedge to the destruction of our public schools? They know very well if we yield this point, we give up, not only that which with us is a great principle, but the entire struggle for our excellent common school system. It is because of this fact that they mean, not only to insist upon their demand, but to use all available means to secure it. This effort of Rome must be met by every lover of our juvenile institutions. It must be met manfully and firmly—met in the name of education, liberty, and humanity. We owe it to ourselves, to our children, and to our country. The rising generation, and all succeeding generations, must be educated. Never was there a time when the education of the masses was more essential to our welfare than now. Upon the general diffusion of knowledge depend the permanency and safety of our free institutions. Let our common school system go down before the sturdy blows of Popery, and an intellectual night settle down upon the masses, and our doom is sealed. In vain, then, will our fields bloom, the seasons smile, the earth pour plenty into our store-houses, and the Stars and Stripes float on every sea. A plague spot will be upon us, solemnly warning us of desolation. Ichabod will then have been written upon our walls, and our glory departed. But this must never be. Our public schools must be preserved at all hazards. The school funds must be kept inviolable for school purposes only. If sects wish sectarian schools let them have them and support them. Here we take our position, and here we stand.

CHAPTER VII.

Romanism versus Bible.

THAT the Bible was intended by its Divine Author to be read and studied by mankind seems so manifest from the very nature and design of a revelation, that it becomes a matter of profound astonishment, that any church organization should ever have doubted it. And, yet, the Roman Catholic Church has not only professed to have doubted it, but has denied the Word of God to the people, and has enforced the prohibition by imprisonments, tortures, and death. All this has been done time and again, and has become the settled policy of the Romish hierarchy, and that, too, in the very face of the plainest injunctions of Holy Writ. " And these words which I command thee this day *shall be in thine heart; and thou shalt teach them diligently unto thy children*, and shalt talk to them when thou sittest in thine house, and when thou walkest by the way, and when thou liest down, and when thou risest up," etc. The Psalmist, speaking of a good man, says: " *His delight is in the law of the Lord, and in His law doth he meditate day and night.*" Paul says: " *Let the word of Christ dwell in you richly* in all wisdom." The Bereans were commended, because, having received the Word with all readiness of mind, they *searched the Scriptures daily*," etc. Paul says, "What things were *written* aforetime were *written for our learning*," etc. And a greater than all these, even Jesus Christ himself, says: "*Search the Scriptures*, for in them ye think ye have eternal life, and they testify of me."

And yet, with all of these solemn injunctions of high heaven to read and search this Sacred Book, and to give it to every creature, until it shall become incorporated in the literature of all nations, full in view, Papal Rome has waged a most terrible and unceasing war against both the circulation and reading of the Scriptures.

Even as far back as the seventh century, the Bible was not only sadly neglected by both bishops and priests, but it was declared to be inferior in authority to many mere human compositions, that answered the purpose of the Roman pontiffs far better in extending their ghostly power. The Bible in use among the Romans was the Latin Vulgate, which, as the Latin became obsolete, the Vulgate Bible became less and less understood, until, perhaps, not one in a hundred could read it at all. This fact, instead of being a matter of regret upon the part of the Romish hierarchy, actually became a subject of joy. Pope Gregory VII., in the eleventh century, gave thanks to Almighty God that the people were unable to read the Bible, as the Latin had become a dead language.* The first translation from the Vulgate ever made was in the twelfth century, when the four Gospels were translated into French through one Peter Waldo, which brought on him and his associates such a storm of Popish fury that they were compelled to flee for their lives. In 1229, the Council of Toulouse, in its fourteenth canon, "forbids the laity to have in their possession any copy of the books of the Old and New Testament, except the Psalter, and such portions of them as are contained in the Breviary, or the Hours of the Virgin, and most strictly forbids these works in the vulgar tongue." The Council of Tarracone, convened in 1242, ordered all vernacular versions (all versions readable by the people), to be brought to the bishop to be *burned*, in the following language:

"We also decree that *no one shall keep the books of the Old or New Testament in the Roman tongue;* and should any one be in possession of such books, *he must deliver them up to the bishop of the place* TO BE BURNED, within eight days after the publication of this article, and unless he do this, be he a priest or a layman, he shall be suspected of heresy until he shall have cleared himself."†

In the fourteenth and fifteenth centuries similar prohibitions were made from time to time,

* Epist. vii : 2. † Giessler's Text Book of Ecc. His., Vol. II., p. 392.

in different countries, by bishops and ecclesiastical convocations.

The reading or searching of the Scriptures has been as persistently opposed by the Romish Church as though the Bible was one of the worst books to be found.

The Council of Trent in their *Index Expurgatorius*, which was sanctioned by Pope Clement VII. in 1595, says: "Inasmuch as it is manifest from experience that if the Holy Bible translated into the vulgar tongue be INDISCRIMINATELY ALLOWED to every one, the temerity of men will cause *more evil than good* to arise from it, it is on this point referred to the judgment of the bishops or inquisitors, who *may* by the advice of the priests or confessors, *permit the reading of the Bible translated in the vulgar tongue by Catholic authors, to those persons whose faith and piety they apprehend will be augmented and not injured by it;* and this *permission* they must have IN WRITING. But if any shall have the *presumption* to READ or POSSESS it *without any such written permission, he shall not receive absolution until he have first delivered up such Bible to the ordinary.*"*

Here it is seen that by the highest authority in the Romish Church, the Council and Pope combined, the Bible is forbidden to be circulated among the masses; and that if any one

* Council of Trent, Sess. XXV.

should venture to read it without a written permit from a bishop, he is to be subjected to one of the severest ecclesiastical penalties of the church.

Quesnel, a Roman Catholic reformer, had said : " It is useful and necessary at all times, in all places, and for all sorts of persons, to study and know the spirit, piety, and mysteries of the Scriptures. The reading of the holy Scriptures is for every body." For this Quesnel was denounced, and these sentiments were formally condemned by Pope Clement XI. in 1731, in his famous *Bull Unigenitus*, as "*false, captious, shocking, offensive to pious ears, scandalous, pernicious, rash, seditious, impious, blasphemous,*" etc.

It would seem as though the Pope had lost all patience with the advocacy of Bible reading by the people, and that he was utterly at a loss for language sufficiently bitter and vindictive to express his horror and indignation against the recommendation for the people to read the Bible. The only charges against the Waldenses, against whom the fierceness of Popish fury raged with unabated cruelty for long weary years, until their country was made a desolation, and, according to the historian, more than a million were destroyed; the only charges against this people were that they read and circulated the Scriptures among the common people, and refused to do homage to Popery. For reading and circulating the Word of Life, and worshiping God according to the dictates of their own consciences, they were subjected to all the horrors of the Inquisition. Large armies were raised and commissioned to extirpate them from the face of the earth. By the ax, by fire, by the sword, and by various other barbarities, did Rome urge on the terrible work of extermination. Hundreds, in the dead of winter, fled to the mountains to escape the fury of their pursuers, where they perished with cold and hunger. But all these things were heroically endured by these faithful witnesses, rather than give up their Bibles.

When Bible Societies were established, in the beginning of the present century, they found in Romanism a most determined foe. This move of Protestantism to circulate the Scriptures immediately called forth an encyclical from Pope Pius VII. on the 26th of June, 1816, against all Bible Societies, as follows: " We have been truly shocked at this most crafty device (Bible Societies), by which the very foundations of religion are undermined. We have deliberated upon the measures proper to be adopted by our pontifical authority, in order to remedy and *abolish this pestilence*, as far as possible,—this defilement of the faith so imminently dangerous to souls. It becomes episcopal duty that you the primate) first of all expose the *wickedness of this nefarious scheme. It is evident from experience that the Holy Scriptures, when circulated in the vulgar tongue, have through the temerity of men, produced more harm than benefit.* Warn the people entrusted to your care, that they fall not into the *snares prepared for their everlasting ruin.*"*

Is it not truly astonishing that the acknowledged head of the Roman Catholic Church should ever have been betrayed into such abominable utterances as the above? If such sentiments were confined to any *one* of the Popes, charity would lead us to regard him as under the influence of some cerebral eccentricity. But this is not the case. It is but one of many such warnings to Papists against the Bible and Bible Societies. Pope Leo XII. in his encyclical letter dated May 5, 1824, expresses himself thus: " You are aware, venerable brothers, that a Society vulgarly called BIBLE SOCIETY, audaciously spreads itself over all the land, and that in contempt of the traditions of the holy fathers, and against the celebrated decree of the Council of Trent, they aim, with all their strength and every means, to translate, or rather corrupt the Holy Scriptures in the vulgar tongue of every nation,"† etc.

---

* Dowling's His. of Rom. book ix. chap. iii. § 24.
† Bower's His. of the Popes,—Leo XII.

The same hostility to the circulation of the Scriptures was expressed by Pope Gregory XVI. in 1832.

Nor were these encyclicals of Popes and decrees of Councils against the reading and circulation of the Scriptures unmeaning or idle ceremonies. They were not only clothed with the acknowledged and regularly constituted authority of the Church, but were frequently enforced by the infliction of the most horrible tortures, and even death itself, upon such as dared to read the Bible according to the command of God.

This determination upon the part of the Romish hierarchy to withhold the Word of Life from the people, seems to be fully carried out in Roman Catholic countries. In the Papal States, where the Pope has every thing his own way, without let or hindrance, the prohibition against the reading and circulation of the Scriptures is most rigidly enforced. Dr. Murry, who, when he was there, took special pains to investigate this matter, says: " *There is no Bible in Rome.* I made many inquiries there for a Bible, but without success. *The people have no Bible. They know nothing about it.* An intelligent man of fifty told me that he never saw one. *Multitudes of the priests know nothing about it.* And when asked why they have none for sale, the booksellers will tell you that it is prohibited. Captain Packenham, once a banker in the city, and a most respectable gentleman and devout Christian, *is now in banishment for circulating the Scriptures there* during the short existence of the Republic." Is it, therefore, strange that the people of that oppressed and priest-ridden country should be noted for their ignorance of the spirituality of that worship demanded by Christ, and their deplorable superstition?

The Rev. J. A. Clark, of Philadelphia, writing from Rome, says: " The Bible in Rome is a strange and rare book. The only edition authorized to be sold here is in fifteen large volumes, which are filled with Popish comments. Of course none but the rich can purchase a copy. Indeed, very few of the common people here know what we mean by a Bible."

Not many years ago a student of Maynooth College, Ireland, by the name of O'Beirne, was expelled that institution for persisting in reading the Bible, just as though the Bible was the worst book in the world. A student of that college may read whatever is most offensive to purity and piety in the ancient classics, and even the obscene detailed instructions of Dens' Theology, without any danger of expulsion, but if he reads the Bible he is dismissed with dishonor.

A Galway newspaper, in the same country,

some time since denounced, by name, two Protestant clergymen as *reptiles*, and advised that they should be *trampled upon for having held a Bible meeting*, and distributed this sacred volume. It speaks of them as a *hell inspired junta of incarnate fiends*, and says: "*If the devil himself came upon earth, he would assume no other garb than that of one of these biblicals.*" The editor adds, with evident warmth: "*The Biblical junta must be put down.*" How strange it is that Papists will permit themselves to be so carried away by such a storm of passion against the Bible as to be betrayed into such absurd and malicious utterances. What must be the condition of that mind and heart that can characterize the circulation of a heaven inspired book as a hell-inspired work? This is about a match for the blasphemous charge of the Jews against Christ: "He casteth out devils through Beelzebub."

The Rev. Mr. Bliss, who not long since attended a meeting of the Bithynia Evangelical Union, at Mooradchoi, in Bithynia (some one hundred and fifty miles from Constantinople) says: "Five or six years ago the Bible in the modern Armenian was introduced among this people. The priest warned the people against the book, and so wrought upon their ignorance and superstition as to raise a storm of persecution against all who favored the introduction of the Word of God. When the servants of Christ visited the place they lodged them in a sort of town hall, and were allowed no intercourse with the people." So severe and determined was the persecution against Bible readers, that the first Protestant convert, he adds, "*was assassinated.*"

Rev. J. Spaulding, writing from South America, where Romanism has had every thing her own way ever since the conquest of that country, says: "The Bible, to an astonishing and almost incredible extent, is a new book, and a real curiosity in this country." The same is true of Spain, Portugal, Belgium, Austria, and other Papal countries.

Roman Catholics openly confess that they have no confidence in Bibles or Bible reading. One of their papers, the New York *Tablet*, in speaking of the work of our Bible and Tract Societies during the past year, says:

"The three-quarters of a million of dollars received by the Society during the year resulted in the printing and scattering abroad of a vast number of copies of the Protestant Scriptures, with not the slightest certainty that even a soul was converted to God, or made to abandon the ways of iniquity, because of these books! Tens of thousands of these we know are never read by any one, and of those that are read how many produce effects the very opposite to what God desires of his creatures?"

Was there ever a falsehood more glaring than

the above, that Bibles do no good? Let any one compare the United States with South America, or Mexico, and he will see the mighty contrast between the land of Bibles and the land of no Bible. Modern history is replete with demonstrations of the marvellous influence of the Bible upon nations, in enlightening and elevating them, and the *Tablet* knows it. As Protestantism owes its all to the Bible, and is making its headway against Romanism through the circulation of the Scriptures, they naturally seek to keep them from the people. Hence Romish priests have often burned and destroyed Bibles which they have found in the hands of their people, as was done in the town of Champlain, N. Y. on the 27th of October, 1842.

A little over a year ago intelligence was received of an outbreak of Romanists against the Protestants of Puebla, Mexico, because of the attempt of the latter to circulate the Scriptures. " For some time," says the *Tribune,* " there has been a Bible agency there, and a small but growing Protestant society. On Sunday, November 28th, when but ten of the congregation —all men—had entered the room, they were attacked, as if by concert, by a large mob, and four who remained, and attempted to close the room against the invaders, were seized, beaten and stoned. *Three boxes of Bibles* and other books were *burned,* and $60, received for Bibles, were stolen. *The mob was led by two priests of the Mexican Catholic Church.* Surely comment is unnecessary. These facts speak for themselves.

Some years ago the Christian Alliance was formed in New York, the object of which was to circulate the Bible without note or comment, in the prevailing language of the different Papal countries where the sacred Scriptures were almost unknown. The avowed purposes of this society produced the greatest consternation in Rome. And in order, if possible, to counteract the efforts of the society, Pope Gregory XVI., on the 8th of May, 1844, issued a bull against the association and its object, from which we quote the following:

"Let all know, then, the enormity of the sin against God and his church which they are guilty of who dare associate themselves with any of these societies, or abet them in any way. Moreover, *we confirm* and *renew* the decrees recited above, delivered in former times by apostolic authority, *against} the publication, distribution, reading, and possession of the books of the Holy Scriptures* translated into the vulgar tongue."

Mark you! what the Pope declares as an enormous sin against God is not merely the publication, reading, and possession of Protestant Bibles, but "the Holy Scriptures translated into the vulgar tongue," either by Romanists or Protestants. By whoever, or however translated into the common language of the people, their publication, distribution, reading, or possession, constitutes a crime of such fearful enormity, that the Pope is shocked beyond measure at its contemplation.

That I do not misrepresent the case, is evident from the injunction of Pope Benedict XIV., which reads:

"No version whatever should be suffered to be read but those which should be approved of by the Holy See, accompanied with notes derived from the writings of the Holy Fathers, or other learned and Catholic authors."*

From this it is evident that Bibles of their own translation, of their own making, although approved by the Pope himself, would not be permitted to be put in circulation without accompanying notes to teach, what the Bible alone, by whoever translated, will not teach, namely, the peculiar doctrines and practices of Popery. Hence Romish priests and bishops have consigned Roman Catholic translations to the flames as well as others.

A case of this kind occurred in Chili, South America, a few years ago. A Roman Catholic version of the New Testament had been printed by the American Bible Society in Spanish without note or comment, and circulated there. An agent of the society in writing to the secretary,

* Dowling's Romanism, book ix., chap. iii, § 25.

relates the following process of burning their own translations :

"On Sabbath evening, the time fixed for the sacrilegious conflagration, a procession was formed having the curate at the head, and conducted with the usual pomp, the priest kneeling a few moments at each corner of the square, and placing a large crucifix upon the ground. During the afternoon a fire had been kindled for the purpose, I was told by several bystanders, of burning heretical books which ridiculed the mass and confession ; and among the number was mentioned the New Testament. A guard of soldiers prevented me from examining them separately, but I stood sufficiently near to discover that the greater part were copies of the New Testament, issued by the American Bible Society. As the flames ascended, increasing in brightness, one of the clergy shouted Viva Deos (Let God reign). * * * The outrage was public, and instead of being disowned, was *openly defended, it was said, in compliance with the decree of an infallible council.* The Scriptures burned were of the approved Spanish version, *translated from the vulgate by a Spanish Roman Catholic bishop.* They were *New Testaments*, too, so the plea that the apocrypha was excluded, could not be urged. They were portions of their own acknowledged word of God, because in the vulgar tongue and without notes, solemnly committed to the flames."*

While the Papal hierarchy have had societies for almost everything else, they have never yet had one for the circulation of the Bible of any description, not even among their own people ;

---

* Dowling's His. of Rom., book ix., chap. iii, § 27.

and consequently, perhaps, not one Roman Catholic in fifty has a Bible of any kind. The truth is, as we have seen, the Romish Church dare not trust even her own people with their own translations of the Bible, without authorized Papal notes accompanying the text, lest they should renounce Popery and become heretics.

CHAPTER VIII.

Our Public Schools a Necessity to the Perpetuity of our Free Institutions.

THAT Romanists should hate our free school system, or covertly seek its destruction, is not to be wondered at, when we consider what has been their policy and practice in reference to general education, and especially State education, in all lands, where their policy and practice could be fairly and safely developed. But that they should have so soon and so openly and boldly commenced their opposition to them, was hardly to have been expected; much less that they should assume a defiant tone and denounce our public school system as "from the devil." But we must remember that Popery has always been bold and obtrusive, and that according to her own teachings for the last thousand years, Protestants have no rights or institutions, that the Romish hierarchy are bound to patronize or respect. Consequently, we might just as well understand this first as last, that it is utterly useless to attempt to so modify our public schools as to satisfy Romanists. They do not so much demand their modification as their destruction. While the glory of Protestants is universal education, the glory of Rome is universal ignorance. "Public schools must be put down," is the shiboleth by which the orthodoxy of Papists is being tested. "The Public or Common School System," says the *Tablet*, " in New York city, is a *swindle* on the people, an *outrage* on justice, a foul disgrace in matters of *morals*, and that it imports for the legislature to abolish it forthwith."

That the general education and intelligence of the masses are vastly important as safeguards to our free institutions, there can be no reasonable doubt. A Republican government especially must depend upon an intelligent basis for its stability. The experience of past ages goes to demonstrate that just in proportion as general education is encouraged, and knowledge diffused throughout the various ranks of society, just in the same ratio may we calculate upon the growth, development and permanency of the God-given rights of free thought, free speech, a free press, and liberty to worship God according to the dictates of conscience. An ignorant constituency may do for a despotic government, but never for a republic. Consequently we see as a rule, intelligence and liberty arranging themselves on the one side, and ignorance and despotism on the other. Their relations and affinities are such that they usually live and die together.

When the legislative, judicial, and executive

departments of the government are all in the hands of the people, as they are in the United States, it is plain the masses must be educated in order to secure an intelligent administration of the affairs of the nation. For this purpose our public school system has been instituted, and to secure the permanency and prosperity of our free institutions, we believe it to be absolutely essential. While it has been affirmed that "an enlightened people can never be enslaved," it is also equally evident that an ignorant people are not capable of self-government. Such generally are used as mere tools by designing demagogues to secure spoils and power. To guard against this danger we must have common intelligence and common morality, and these principally depend upon common schools. Select educational institutions may be ever so good, yet they necessarily have a limited scope, and, therefore, must have a limited influence. Our common schools are a necessity. Our principal danger lies with the ignorant portions of community. They furnish the material for riots, lawless violence, and insubordination. Among them are seen the very worst passions of depraved humanity, like some foul pestilence corrupting, blighting and desolating all around them. From their ranks, our prisons, penitentiaries and scaffolds are principally supplied with victims. Such are the legitimate results

Public Schools a Necessity. 97

of neglected childhood; for this class is made up of uneducated children grown up to manhood. To lessen this dangerous element, and to, if possible, ultimately destroy it, we need our common schools to educate their children to become better members of society. If we give up our common school system, we abandon the only means by which we can hope to remedy this gigantic evil. At no period in our history could we so illy afford to risk the destruction of our public school system as now. The recent slaveholders' rebellion resulted in the emancipation of some 4,000,000 of human beings who have recently been admitted to citizenship, and its privileges, in accordance with the principles of our government. Against these 4,000,000 all schools were closed by the laws of the unnatural institution that enslaved them. Even the elementary education of slaves was made a crime to be punished with fines and imprisonments. In consequence of this oppressive system, at the time of their emancipation they were deplorably ignorant. Much has already been done to educate them, but more remains to be done. They must be educated to render them intelligent and virtuous. Without education they are dangerous both to government and society. Instead of wondering at the many instances of lawlessness and violence that have occurred among them, the wonder is that, in view of their illiterate condition, there has not been more. But the safety and welfare of society demand that they shall be educated, but how can this be done without our public school system being continued and extended?

This must be done. These juvenile institutions must be made national; not only free for all, but extended to all. They should be inaugurated in every State and Territory where they do not already exist. The General government and the State governments should speedily make the necessary appropriations. There can be no better investments. I doubt not but that if Congress, instead of having appropriated since 1806 only about $8,000,000 for educational purposes among the Indians, had appropriated $100,000,000; that then, instead of having had to appropriate during the above time $500,000,000 for war purposes among them, as they have done, $200,000,000 would have been ample for this latter purpose, and thus the sum of $200,000,000 saved to the nation; besides having vastly improved the character of the Indians, and their good feeling towards us. Our public school system is absolutely indispensable to the permanency and welfare of our free institutions.

In despotic governments the great object to be achieved with the masses is to make them good subjects. This can be accomplished in most cases better without general education than with. But in a Republic, such as we have in these United States, the case is far otherwise. Hence, upon us devolves the higher responsibility of so educating the people that they may not only make good subjects, but what is vastly more important, good *sovereigns;* for here all power originates with the people and returns to them. But how can this be done without general education, without our free scnools? What colleges are to aristocratic classes that govern in the old world, common schools are to us. Colleges are essential to high culture, and can never be dispensed with under any circumstances, but after all they are not so essential to us as are public schools.

Says Horace Mann, in a speech delivered in Boston some time since :

"With the change in the organic structure of our government, there should have been corresponding changes in all public measures and institutions. For every dollar given by the wealthy, or by the State, to colleges, to cultivate the higher branches of knowledge, a hundred should have been given for primary education. For every acre of land bestowed upon an academy, a province should have been granted to common schools. Select schools for select children should have been discarded, and *universal* education should have joined hands with universal suffrage."

Until our system of education is co-extensive

with our system of suffrage, we have no assurance of the stability of our free institutions.

Our danger is also largely increased by the ceaseless tide of European emigration that is yearly pouring its tens and hundreds of thousands upon our shores, shackled with ignorance and Popish superstitions. This vast foreign element must be Americanized into the life forces of the nation. We greatly need the influence of our common schools to unite our various nationalities into one homogeneous mass. There is a wonderful power in these schools to fuse nationalities, even while personal idiosyncracies are preserved. Our peril is sufficiently great in the absorption of this immense foreign element, without allowing our public school system to be destroyed to please Romanists or any body else. To us is committed the important work of constructing an individual civilization, having its own peculiar and well-defined characteristics and essential features. We are under the most solemn obligations to retain, use, and strengthen every institution, and instrumentality that can be pressed into the service, to assimilate and lay under contribution the various types of civilization, whether Christian or Pagan, that are pouring in upon us from Europe and Asia. We owe this as a sacred duty to ourselves, to our children, to posterity, and to God; and in view of the immense future emigration of heathens from Asia, and Romanists from Europe, we have a gigantic task before us. The more antagonistic their views, feelings, customs, prejudices, theories, and opinions to our institutions, the greater the necessity that influences should be used to mould them into harmonious co-operation. To accomplish this, no better agency exists than our public schools. The Roman hierarchy understand this; and because they hate our civil and religious institutions, they are resolved on the destruction of these schools. The same reason, however, that leads them to seek their destruction, should stimulate us to defend them.

Instead of parleying with Rome, as to whether we shall have free schools for all or not; whether we shall stand by the principles adopted by our fathers, and which lie at the foundation of Protestantism, or cravenly bow to the dictation of the Pope, the avowed enemy of all that we as Protestants love and cherish, it would be far better to resolve to sustain them at all hazards, in the face of opposition and combinations of every form.

In fact, we believe it would be still better to secure the passage of an act by the legislatures of the several States, compelling every child between certain ages to attend some school, either public, ecclesiastical, or charitable. Such a law, if enforced, would go far toward lessening juvenile crime, and stopping the growth of an ignorant and dangerous class to law and order.

That the State has a right to force the education of its subjects, there can be no reasonable doubt. Compulsory education is certainly the right of the State, as much as conscription or compulsory service is the right of the State in time of war. Of the latter no one questions the right of the State for a moment; why should they question the former? Would it be harder to parents for the State to compel their children to attend school, than to compel their sons to bear arms in the defense of our country? If the common school is the mightiest fortification of the commonwealth, there can be no reason why the children should not be compelled to attend.

The secret of the enormous power, energy and enterprise of Prussia, as developed in her present conflict with France, is undoubtedly in a great measure to be attributed to the superior intelligence of her people. This is owing to her comprehensive plan of popular education. This system is compulsory, by which every child between the ages of seven and fourteen, who is not an invalid or idiot, is compelled by law to attend school. The vast superiority of the Germans over the French, who have no such system, is a sufficient comment upon the advantages of general compulsory education.

Public Schools a Necessity. 103

"I should not be candid," says Mr. Mundella, in his Cooper Institute speech, "if I did not frankly tell you that North Germany and Switzerland excel you in the thoroughness and the universality of their systems; and this, I believe, is entirely owing to the fact, that, in those countries, the parent has not the right to deprive the child of the excellent training which the State has provided. When the parent fails in his duty, the State stands in *loco parentis;* and this is what you chiefly need to perfect your educational system."

We are no longer the most generally educated people in the world. Others are outstripping us in this respect in consequence of having adopted the compulsory plan. This has prepared the way for the rapid strides of Prussia to the leadership of Europe. And if we would act wisely we must adopt the same system, otherwise we must fall in the rear of more vigorous and enterprising nations.

That a compulsory system of education is necessary in these United States, is made abundantly evident by the recently published statistics on education by the General government. From this document it appears that in twenty-two States where there were 5,695,916 children enrolled in the schools, there was but an average attendance of 3,377,069. At the same time there is a total average absence in these twenty-two States from the public schools of the enormous number of 4,843,568 children of school age. This is truly alarming, and calls loudly for enforced education throughout the land.

Now who does not believe that compulsory education would be an improvement upon our present system? At all events, let there be no steps taken backward upon this question. Let there be no hesitation upon the part of Protestants, as to whether our public school system shall be maintained, and intelligence made the basis of our government, or whether we shall get down upon our knees in the dust to the Romish hierarchy, and tamely submit to the destruction of these schools, and the enthronement of their system of ignorance, superstition, and despotism.

CHAPTER IX.

A Moral Element of Instruction is Essential to the Success of our Public School System and the Welfare of the Nation.

IN the education of children two very dissimilar systems of school training have been adopted at various times and in different countries. One is that in which the moral faculties are altogether neglected; where the mind is merely crowded with facts, theories, and speculations, without any reference to their higher and philosophical relations to the Supreme Being. The other is that in which the moral nature of the child is recognized as an essential element of his very existence, and which must be especially cared for in the training process.

The former, which aims only to secure bare intellectual culture, can never be accepted by a Christian nation as a suitable system of education without self-stultification and peril. Such an institution overlooks the most important part of man's nature. Children are endowed with moral faculties as well as adults, and these can never be neglected by the State with impunity. As the moral nature is higher than the physical or intellectual, its culture and development are of paramount consideration. The system that fails to impress the mind with moral truths and reflections, however well it may succeed in imparting whatever is embraced in a common school education, or even in the higher grades of literature, so as to make its pupils familiar with the entire round of classical and mathematical training, would leave its work but half completed. A knowledge of exponents and co-efficients, of angles and parallaxes, of sines and co-sines, of tangents and secants, etc., can never be made to supply the place of moral culture. A man may be distinguished for his literary attainments, the profundity of his knowledge, and his metaphysical acuteness, and still be a villain at heart, a monster in crime.

Bourne has very fitly said; "The foundation of character is laid in the moral nature. The heart is exercised while the mind is yet just unfolding its earliest power. The child loves before he reasons, and exhibits anger before he has learned to utter his first monosyllables. His moral powers are in action long before his judgment has begun to discriminate between right and wrong. It is only when the mind, by years of education and a force of character developed out of the moral nature, has learned to act in certain directions, that the man may be at all claimed as the subject of simply intellectual convictions. In truth, it may be asserted that no man has ever been a moral man simply by convictions gained by reasoning alone. When truth, honesty, love, temperance, self-denial, can be demonstrated by mathematical problems or purely metaphysical abstractions, we may hope to make men good men and upright citizens by intellectual training alone."*

The latter system therefore becomes an absolute necessity, if we would seek to stimulate and develope the most essential part of man's nature, and thereby promote the happiness of the rising generation and the welfare of the nation. This was well understood by our pilgrim fathers, who have left the impress of their devotion to the development and culture of man's moral nature on all of their civil as well as religious institutions. The idea and necessity of moral culture was necessarily a leading thought with the founders of our nation. They had fled from intolerance and persecution, to these then Western wilds, to worship God according to the dictates of their own consciences. " It is certain," says an early New England writer, " that civil dominion was but the second motive, religion the primary one, with our ancestors coming hither. . . . It was not so much their design to establish religion for the benefit of the State, as civil government for the benefit of religion." Another, a century earlier, testi-

* Wm. Oland Bourne's Hist. of Public Schools, p. 19.

fies that the fathers " came not hither for world, or for land, or for traffic; but for religion, and for liberty of conscience in the worship of God, which was their only design."

This sacred interest, their religion, was their absorbing thought, and was first every where. "As near the law of God as can be," was the instruction of the General Court of Massachusetts, in olden time, to its committee appointed to frame laws for the Commonwealth. No people ever laid the foundations of a government deeper in moral ethics, or broader, upon which they hoped their descendants might build a Christian empire, than did our Puritanic ancestors. They laid the corner-stone of a Christian civilization, upon which should tower up in stately proportions, a spiritual temple. Nothing could be more absurd than the supposition that they did not regard morality as an essential part of education; and nothing would be more unworthy of us as their descendants, the inheritors of their free institutions, than to ignore the necessity of moral culture in our public schools. In all the past, we have, as a people, recognized morality as the basis of all correct education. Shall we do less in the future?

Says Chief Justice Shaw: "The public school system was intended to provide a system of moral training." The moral sense of the nation is

Moral Instruction Essential to Education.

under the influence and control of the teachings of the Bible, and, just to that extent it is ignored, just to that extent is the moral support of the laws undermined, and the community corrupted.

That the whole framework of our government rests upon a distinct recognition of the Bible and morality as founded on the Bible, is abundantly evident every where. If Christianity and the Scriptures are not made the law of the land, how could blasphemy be made a crime? Besides in most if not in all the States, the Legislatures have exempted the Family Bible from executions; have required that every apprentice shall be furnished with a Bible; and that a Bible shall be put into the hands of every inmate of a jail, penitentiary, and reformatory institution, and all this at the public expense. Our courts of justice and halls of legislatures are also supplied with Bibles, and all this on the grounds that religion and morality are essential to good government. Now, if the State has the right, and deems it important in view of its own welfare, to furnish the Bible to the above-named persons and institutions, where would be the reason, or the justice, or utility in withholding the Word of Life from our children in the public schools? Can they be proper in the one case and not in the other? Morality is a political as well as a religious necessity. It is a fundamental—a vital principle, that has been recognized in the structure of our government. For, if the State has no right to insist on the inculcation of morality, then it has no right to lay and solidify the foundation of its own permanence. If it has this right, which cannot be questioned, then it has the right to require and enforce the inculcation of morality in its institutions of learning. Republican governments must have a moral as well as an educated common people. Free schools must be made the factors of morality as well as factors of intelligence. Morality is necessarily involved in the very nature of society, and constitutes the basis of all obligation and constitutional law.

Now as all morality is based upon religion, and as the only religion recognized in this country is the religion of the Bible, it follows that this inspired volume should be the book out of which morality should be inculcated, and therefore the school room is a proper place for the Bible. This blessed book, which constitutes the basis not only of our government, but also the basis of every free, just and prosperous government in the world, should early come in contact with the young to enlighten their minds, impress their hearts, and form their consciences.

Says M. Cousin, in his report upon Public education in Germany, as quoted in *Bibliothe-*

ca Sacra: "The general system of instruction is grounded on the Bible as translated by Luther, the Catechism and Scripture history; and every wise man will rejoice in this; for with three-fourths of the population, morality can be instilled only through the medium of religion. Luther's forcible and popular translation of the Bible is in circulation from one end of Protestant Germany to the other, and has greatly aided in the moral and religious education of the people."

That the infusion of a moral element in the mind and conscience of the nation is essential to its welfare and prosperity, is abundantly attested by past history. We need only to refer to France just previous to her revolution, as an illustration of the necessity of introducing moral instruction into the general system of education. There infidel philosophers prepared a system of godless education. "The design of which was," says Burke, "to abolish the Christian religion under all its forms, whenever the minds of men were prepared for it. These enthusiasts do not scruple to avow their opinion that a State can subsist without any religion better than with one; and that they were able to supply the place of any good which might be in it by a project of their own, and this system they called a civic education."

Well, the plan was fairly tried—the experiment was accordingly made. The Bible was prohibited and banished from all their public institutions of instruction. Every book inculcating its great moral truths shared the same fate. Religion and its ministers were despised, and the temples of religion were closed. What was the result? I cannot state it better than in the language of a certain writer, who says: "The passions of men were let loose, the social ties dissolved, the domestic affections stifled, the foundations of civil society broken up, and a scene of horror ensued which no man can look back to, even at this distance of time, without shuddering at the depravity to which human nature, uninfluenced by religion, may reach even in an enlightened country. So complete was the desolation, that when the storm had subsided, and a committee was sent to Paris by one of the religious societies of London, to ascertain the moral condition of the people, they searched four days in all the bookstores and print shops of Paris, before they could find a single copy of the Bible." The moral degradation—the unbounded licentiousness—the extravagant wickedness—the utter subversion of all that society holds dear, became so constant and universal, that even infidels and atheists became appalled at the wide-spread ruin they had pulled down upon the nation.

"I have consulted," says Rousseau, "our philosophers;

I have perused their books, I have examined their several opinions; I have found them all proud, positive, and dogmatizing, even in their pretended scepticism; knowing every thing, proving nothing, and ridiculing one another; and this last is the only point in which they concur, and in which they are right. Where is the philosopher who for his own glory would not willingly deceive the whole human race? Where is he who in the secret of his heart proposes any other object than his own distinction? The great thing for him is to think differently from other people; under the pretence of being themselves the only people enlightened, they imperiously subject us to their magisterial decisions, and would fain palm upon us, for the true causes of things, the unintelligible systems they have erected in their own heads. While they overturn, destroy and trample under foot all that mankind reveres; snatch from the rich and great the only curb that can restrain their passions, tear from the heart all remorse of vice, all hopes of virtue, they still boast themselves the benefactors of mankind."

Now, are we, with these terrible facts before us, prepared to adopt that policy that proved to be so ruinous to them? Shall we embrace measures directly tending to rear up and multiply infidels and atheists in our midst? Shall we, to satisfy the unreasonable demands of Romanists, consent to withhold the Bible from some seven millions of children in our public schools, and thereby give public and official recognition and sanction to the Romish dogma that the Bible is not a fit book for the common people? Shall we basely consent to make our schools godless schools, and thereby violate our consciences, and offend our Maker? Are we as Protestants prepared for all this? Yet this is precisely what the Romanists would have us do if they could. They charge our public schools as "godless schools," and then do their worst to make them such. They would have us not only to expel the Bible therefrom, but every book in which Christianity is taught or recommended, and then they would rejoice at the moral desolation they had made. If any one doubts this, let him ponder the following extract from the *Western Watchman* of St. Louis, a Roman Catholic paper, in reference to the expulsion of the Bible from the schools of Cincinnati, as quoted by the *Christian World:*

"The much vexed question of Bible reading in the public schools of Cincinnati is at length settled. . . . The resolution of the Board is sweeping; and not only is the Bible excluded, and all hymns, prayers, and whatever else savors of religion. Books, too, in which Christianity is taught, must be replaced, or expurgated, and no vestige of religious truth can be allowed to disgrace the hallowed precincts of the school room. Protestants are found for the first time in the history of our State school system, taught that no religion, not even that weak dilution of it which we call Puritanism, is compatible with the well being of their much extolled institution. Our school instruction must be purely materialistic. If the name of the Author of Christianity is mentioned at all, He must be spoken of as one of the men who figured prominently in history, as we would speak of Mahomet, Julius Cæsar or Napoleon. Under no circumstances may we hint to the child that the great preacher and teacher was God. We may not even tell him that he has a soul, or that there is any code of morality outside the statutes of the city, and the records of the police courts. There must be nothing in the character or surroundings of our schools which might offend a Jew, a Mahommedan, a disciple of Confucius, or a common infidel. Our State has no religion, and our schools can have none."

Such was the prospective moral aspect of the public schools of Cincinnati, for which the editor of the above paper labored, and over which he and other Romanists were jubilant. And be it remembered that such is the fearful character they propose to fix upon all our public schools throughout the land. Let those Protestants who are ready to yield up the Bible and banish it from these institutions for the sake of peace, ask themselves the question, if they are ready to make such a sacrifice, even for the sake of peace?

The unreasonable demand of Romanists against the inculcation of moral truths and precepts, under the pretense of guarding our schools against the danger of sectarianism, will appear the more transparent when we take into consideration the fact, that no such vigilance is manifested to protect our schools from the dissemination of infidel and atheistic sentiments and publications. These are often disguised under vague and endlessly varying negations, and are therefore the more insidious and fatal. They most adroitly and covertly take upon themselves the honored names of literature and philosophy. Even the nonsensical vagaries of Huxley, that bring a man out of a monkey, and the monkey out of a fungus, and the fungus out of a monad, are presented under the specious plea of science.

Now, in view of these facts, can any one doubt the wisdom or the duty of seeking to fortify the minds of our children against these and kindred forms of errors that are sure to meet them sooner or later, by insisting that positive morality shall constitute an important element in our public school instruction?

Every form of school training that aims only to cultivate the mind, that utterly ignores the moral nature of the child, comes far short of securing the important ends of a proper education. In 1842 an English court decided that the courts of England "Will not sanction any system of education in which religion is not included." And in course of hearing the court remarked that "a scheme of education without religion would be worse than mockery."

Professor Stowe, in his report on Elementary Instruction in Europe, says:—

"In regard to the necessity of moral instruction and the beneficial influence of the Bible in schools, the testimony was no less explicit and uniform. I inquired of all

Moral Instruction Essential to Education. 117

classes of teachers, and men of every grade of religious faith, instructors in common schools, high schools, and schools of art, of professors in colleges, universities, and professional seminaries in cities and in the country, in places where there was a uniformity and in places where there was a diversity of creeds, and I never found but one reply, and that was, to leave the moral faculty uninstructed was to leave the most important part of the human mind undeveloped, and to strip education of almost everything that can make education valuable; and that the Bible, independently of the interest attending it, as containing the most ancient and influential writings ever recorded by human hands, and composing the religious system of almost the whole of the civilized world, is, in itself, the best book that can be put into the hands of children to interest, to exercise, and to unfold their intellectual and moral powers. Every teacher whom I consulted repelled with indignation that moral instruction is not proper for schools; and spurned with contempt the allegations that the Bible cannot be introduced into common schools without encouraging a sectarian bias in the matter of teaching; an indignation and contempt which I believe will be fully participated in by every high-minded teacher in Christendom."

The legitimate end of education, so far as the State is concerned, is unquestionably to make good citizens. But how can good citizenship be secured without the inculcation of a strong and vigorous moral sentiment in the minds of the people? And certainly there is no period of life when this can be better commenced than in childhood. Nor is there any better book than that which is the fountain of all religious knowledge, and the source of all morality. Hence no greater blunder could be committed by those entrusted with the education of the rising generation than the banishment of the Bible from our public schools. A high-toned morality among the people is essential to the stability of a Republican government, and there certainly can be no better time to lay the foundation for such than in childhood; and certainly no better book for such a purpose than the Bible. Says Dr. R. W. Clark, of Albany:

"If the Bible is taken from these schools, and all religious and moral instruction suppressed, and the millions of voices that have been accustomed to sing religious songs are suppressed, we relinquish the greatest power that Almighty God has placed in our hands to mould aright the elements that endanger the Republic. Instead of thereby saving civil liberty, we take the first step towards its destruction. Instead of preserving religious toleration, we pave the way for intoleration. Instead of strengthening the State, we demolish one of its main pillars, and encourage the foes of liberty and the Bible to go on until every pillar and column is shattered, and the whole fabric, which has been so long our boast and glory, is level with the ground."

Very much in this strain is the language of Dr. Budington, who says:

"It is historically true that our country's free institutions came from the religion of the country. Americans did not become freemen first, and Christians afterwards, but Christians first. And the power that created, is the

Moral Instruction Essential to Education. 119

only power that can preserve. If any one doubts this, let him look at Europe. The history of the birth and growth of liberty on this side of the ocean, is wonderfully supplemented by the history of attempts to sustain free institutions on that side of the ocean. Why is French republicanism not a success? Every one says, because the French are not fit for a republic. But why are they not fit? Is not the answer inevitable? They are not self-governed. They are atheistic, and religionless. And if anything is demonstrable, it is that a republic cannot be made to rest upon an atheistic population. It needs public conscience; it rests upon a recognition of the government of God. Hence republicanism, without Christianity, is mere selfishness, and as hollow and short-lived as selfishness always is. Men without religion talk of rights, not of duties. But there are no rights, which do not create and live in duties. Self-government in the individual implies subjection to the government of God, and self-government in a nation implies as much. It needs for its working and maintenance, the Sabbath, the Bible."

The plea sometimes urged even by those who believe in the necessity of moral culture, that the places for the religious instruction of children are their homes, the Sabbath schools, and places of worship where parents, Sabbath school teachers and pastors can cultivate and train their moral powers according to their own creed or liking, is far more specious in appearance than sound in philosophy. While all this is very good so far as it goes, and is vastly important, it is nevertheless too circumscribed and imperfect in its availability to meet all cases.

If all children were blessed with religious parents who would seek to bring them up in the fear of God, and who would teach them to keep his commandments, or who would place them under the influences of Sabbath schools and churches, we could better afford to dispense with moral lessons in our public schools; but the case is far otherwise. In tens of thousands of instances the only chance there is for children to receive any moral instruction at all is in our public schools. Thousands of parents are not qualified to teach their children in consequence of their own ignorance or disinclinations; while thousands of others are utterly disqualified by intemperate habits, criminal practices and the most revolting degradation. In many instances, their wretched offsprings are taught, especially in our large cities, from early life to beg and lie and steal to obtain a scanty subsistence. In Sabbath schools they are never seen. No religious instruction can ever reach them directly from these or kindred institutions. To the public schools alone must we look to impress their minds with moral truths and individual responsibilities. While the firesides, the Sabbath schools, and sanctuaries of worship should be centers of mighty moral forces, ever contributing their share of moral instruction to the rising generation, our public schools should also be required to bring to bear their immense influence in the same direction, so as not only to reimpress the truth that may have been learned elsewhere, but more especially to instruct thousands in the higher duties of life that can be reached in no other way.

To this there certainly can be no valid objection so long as only fundamental principles are taught, upon which all believers in revelation agree—so long as the peculiarities and sectarian dogmas of denominational organizations are excluded; in other words, so long as the Bible, the foundation and source of all moral truth, without note or comment, is made the basis of moral instruction by simply reading judiciously selected lessons from its sacred pages.

CHAPTER X.

The Bible a Suitable Book for our Public Schools.

In the education of children, as we have already shown, nothing is more important than the cultivation and development of the moral faculties. On no other principle can we successfully sustain common school education, so as to insure our national perpetuity. We are to start with the fact, that we are a Christian nation, and that infidelity, heathenism, and all other falseisms must give place to Christianity. If the State were only to aim at refining the taste, and storing the intellect of the rising generation with mere scientific facts and theories, it would leave its work but half completed. It is the business of the State to see to it, that the young are prepared to make good citizens. But they can only be made such as we have seen by a proper education of the moral powers. Their usefulness in society, as well as their happiness, both for time and eternity, greatly depend upon this.

It is therefore necessary that our public schools, so far as practicable, should be furnished with such books for the use of children in connection with their literary training, as will tend to inculcate lessons of sound morality.

And now let me ask what other book is there so well calculated to accomplish this end as the Bible? Where else are the principles of morality and virtue so admirably taught as in the sacred Scriptures? There is no book in all the world that will compare with it in this respect. It is the only infallible standard of divine truth. This matchless volume contains more moral sublimity and beauty than can be found aside from it and its teachings, in the most celebrated libraries of any age or nation. " Bring me the book," said Sir Walter Scott, when dying. When asked " What book?" he replied: " Oh! why ask me what book! There is but one book in the world that deserves the name, it is the Bible." Such was the testimony of a man who was familiar with the most renowned publications in the world.

As one of the important objects of education is to form the moral powers and habits of thought, and to give both purity and rectitude to the heart and life, the Bible is absolutely indispensable in our common schools. All past history of all time prove it to be the best book for such purposes. Its efficacy in accomplishing these valuable ends is attested by countless generations.

Look at the matchless spirit of purity which

it breathes in its messages to man. What superior maxims and rules for private, domestic, social and public life are found in the proverbs of Solomon, and the teachings of Christ and His Apostles! What perfect gems of moral instruction are contained in the parables of this wondrous book; such as Jotham's trees, Nathan's ewe-lamb, the Good Samaritan, the unjust steward, the returning prodigal, the widow and the unjust judge, the lost sheep! etc. What heavenly lessons of piety and devotion appear throughout its pages! What poetic strains of enraptured thought, what earnestness of soul and fervency of spirit, are exhibited throughout the psalms of David! There are no songs to be compared to the songs of Zion. Its sublime doctrines and holy precepts make it emphatically a fit companion for all classes. For simplicity, beauty, purity, and power to form the mind and improve the heart, it stands peerless and alone. Here " holy men of old spake and wrote as they were moved by the Holy Ghost." Here only have we a correct and perfect standard of morals, and adequate motives for the observance of the laws of rectitude. Here alone we learn not only the rules of life, but the principles upon which they are founded. Here only have we teachings that take hold on the hidden recesses of the heart, as well as the external life, creating, stimulating, and controlling the emotions and aspirations of the individual to a higher and holier life of godliness.

Even Rousseau, the French infidel, in one of his serious and candid moods, said: "The majesty of the Scriptures strike me with astonishment. Look at the volumes of all the philosophers, with all their pomp, how contemptible do they appear in comparison with this! Is it possible that a book at once so simple and sublime can be the work of man?"

The accomplished scholar and jurist, Sir William Jones, declared that "the Scriptures contain, independently of their divine original, more true sublimity, more exquisite beauty, more important history, pure morality, and finer strains both of poetry and eloquence, than could be collected within the same compass from all other books that were ever composed in any age or in any idiom."

Through its hallowed influences, what iron chains of sin have been broken! what bonds of friendship formed! what vast renovations in society have been achieved! It has prepared savages for society, and given foundations to governments. It has broken the chains of the slave, and overturned the very foundations of a hundred middle walls of partition, and established the common brotherhood of man. If India no longer boasts her annual holocust of thirty thousand widows, it is because the teachings of the Bible have extinguished her unholy fires. Wherever its sacred light has shone, it has reversed the lying verdict of Hindooism, Buddhism, and Mahometanism, that declared women to be soulless, and irreclaimably wicked. In a word, how wonderfully it has elevated our entire race! And how it still enlightens the public mind, instructs the conscience, impresses the heart, and by its marvelous power creates light, love, and glory all around! How many sorrowing hearts has it soothed! How many burdened souls has it released! How many asylums has it reared amid scenes of wretchedness and woe for the suffering and outcast of society! How many millions of hearts has it quickened into tenderness and gushing sympathies! What untold numbers of benevolent impulses it has sent thrilling throughout all the social ranks of society!

There can be no question that the Bible is the very best book from which to impress the minds of our children with their responsibilities, and to unfold and stimulate their moral faculties, and therefore, on this account, must never be expelled from our public schools. No other book can possibly supply its place.

"This book—this holy book, on every line
Marked with the seal of high divinity,—
On every leaf bedewed with drops of love

Divine, and with the eternal heraldry
And signature of God Almighty stamped
From first to last--"

was intended for all classes of mankind. The minds of the young as well as the old need to be enlightened with its sacred truths. It is our solemn duty to see to it that the children of the masses are furnished with a knowledge of the word of life. This fact was fully recognised and insisted upon by the Almighty in his instruction to the Israelites :

"Hear, O Israel! The Lord our God is one Lord, and thou shalt love the Lord thy God with all thine heart, and with all thy soul, and with all thy might. And these words which I command thee this day shall be in thy heart, and thou shalt teach *them diligently unto thy children*, and shalt talk of them when thou sittest in thine house, and when thou walkest by the way, and when thou liest down, and when thou risest up. And thou shalt bind them for a sign upon thy hand, and they shall be frontlets between thine eyes. And thou shalt write them upon the posts of thy house, and on thy gates."

Here it will be observed that the children were, by the direct command of God, to be taught the Scriptures *everywhere*—in all places where they might chance to be. Here is positive authority for reading them to our children gathered in our public schools; for here the greatest number can be reached in a given time. No reason can be given why the Bible should not be read in our public schools that would not apply against it being read to children anywhere. Timothy was commended by Paul because that from a child he had known the holy Scriptures. And so if we would have our children's minds, like Timothy's, imbued with the sublimest system of virtue and morality that is to be found anywhere on earth, let us give them the Bible; and let us see to it that this greatest and best of books is not banished from our system of general education.

CHAPTER XI.

The Literary Character of the Bible an Additional Reason why its Use should be continued in our Public Schools.

THE Bible should be continued in our public schools not only because it is far superior to any other book in the variety of its precepts, the sublimity of its truths, and the purity of its morals; but also because of its high character as a literary work. The historical portions of the Scriptures are justly regarded as unsurpassed either in ancient or modern literature. They open up a long vista in the hoary past where the light of other histories never shine, save by the light of this blessed Book. Here by its sacred pages we are led back to the beginning of time—to creation's mighty work—to the great First Cause; to the mighty Architect of the skies, who with matchless power and wisdom constructed and arranged the vast and complicated machinery of our planetary system, wheel within wheel, in almost endless variety and beauty, and yet in most surprising harmony and adaptation. Here only is to be found an account of the origin of our race, of the primeval condition of man, of his subsequent fall and degradation, of the increase of wickedness that followed his moral corruption, of the great Deluge, of the preservation of Noah and his family, of the repeopling of the earth, of the confusion of tongues, of the founding of ancient empires, etc. Even Professor Huxley is constrained to acknowledge its claims to special recognition in consequence of its high literary character. "Take the Bible as a whole; eliminate, as a sensible lay-teacher would do, all that is not desirable for children to occupy themselves with, and there still remains a vast residuum of moral beauty and grandeur. And then consider the great historical fact that for three centuries this book has been woven into the life of all that is best and noblest in English history; that it is written in the noblest and purest English, and abounds in exquisite beauties of mere literary form; and, finally, that it forbids the veriest hind who never left his village, to be ignorant of the existence of other countries and other civilizations, and of a great past, stretching back to the farthest limits of the oldest nations in the world. By the study of what other book could children be so humanized and made to feel that each figure in the vast historical procession fills, like themselves, but a momentary space in the interval between two eternities?

"On the whole, then, I am in favor of reading the Bible, with such grammatical, geographical, and historical explanations by a lay-teacher as may be needful, with rigid exclusion of any further theological teaching than that contained in the Bible itself."

Indeed no one who has the least candor can help but admit that the mightiest events that have ever occurred in our world's history, are narrated with a surprising simplicity, faithfulness, and majesty. Where is the book to be found that contains stories that equal in touching tenderness and beauty the stories of the Bible? The impressive narrative of Abraham and Isaac, of Jacob and Esau, of Joseph and his brethren, of Naaman the Syrian, of Elijah and Ahab, of the three Hebrews and Nebuchadnezzar, and a host of others equally romantic and impressive. These stories will ever continue to fascinate the young and instruct the old, while the human heart shall love the sublime and beautiful. Said Daniel Webster: "I have read through the entire Bible many times. I now make a practice to go through it once a year. It is the book of all others for lawyers as well as divines, and I pity the man who cannot find in it a rich supply of thought and of rules for his conduct. It fits a man for life. It prepares him for death."

It contains the biographies of the most illustrious personages that have ever lived. It contains the most marvellous prophecies, the most astounding miracles, the most wonderful revelations, the sublimest songs, the most perfect prayers, the purest precepts, the most perfect models of virtue, the most unrivalled beauty of composition, the best maxims of wisdom, the most consistent examples of piety, instances of the strongest faith, the broadest benevolence, the warmest love, the purest emotions, the grandest heroism, the most elevated piety, and the most divine and perfect theology that is to be found any where this side of heaven.

The Bible is not only of great merit as an instructor, but is, according to the best judges, the very best book to use as a model in many branches of literature. For this reason it should occupy a prominent place among the catalogue of text-books to be used in all of our public schools. "It has done more," says R. H. Dana, "to *anchor* the English language in the State, as it then was, than all other books together. The fact that so many millions of each succeeding generation, in all parts of the world where the English language is used, read the same great lessons, in the same words, not only keeps the language anchored where it was in its best state, but it preserves its universality, and frees it from all material provincialisms and *patois*, so that the same words, phrases and idioms are used in London, New York, San Francisco, Australia, China and India. To preserve this unity and steadfastness, the Book of Common Prayer has done much; Shakespeare, Milton, and Bunyan have done much; but the English Bible has done tenfold more than they all."

"No respectable critic," says Dr. Neven, "indeed, from the days of Langinus to our own, has been willing to blast his reputation by the denial that it towers far above all other productions in the high and attractive attributes of thought and style. Even the most enthusiastic admirers of heathen classics have conceded their inferiority to it in the sublime and beautiful, in the descriptive and pathetic, in dignity and simplicity of narrative, in power and comprehensiveness, in depth and variety of thought, and in purity and elevation of sentiment."

Where else shall we find better oratory than in the Bible? Look for instance at the tender, impressive and pathetic pleadings of Judah before Joseph in behalf of Benjamin, in whose sack Joseph's silver cup had been found. In vain shall we look for a higher order of true eloquence among the most renowned pleadings of Greece or Rome. No one can read the noble defence of Paul before Agrippa without being impressed with a sense of genuine eloquence, and of superior diction.

Look at the poetical portions of this blessed Book! What sublimity of thought! What marvels of conception! What master-pieces of imagery! What delicacy of execution—in a word, what perfect gems of untold beauty sparkle and shine with the light of a better world throughout its sacred pages!

It has enlarged the field of scientific investigation, by leading the mind from secondary causes, up, through the elaborate processes of nature to nature's great First Cause. It has revealed a world of beauty in the marvellous harmony which it unfolds as subsisting between the laws of matter and the mind of God. The sciences which occupy so large a place in the intellectual world, when properly considered in relation to their higher and ultimate objects, in a philosophic point of view, are nothing else than the investigation of the power, wisdom, goodness and superintending providences of the Almighty, as displayed in the formation, adaptation and movements of the universe; and where else shall we find so perfect a key to the inner chamber of cause and effect as in the Bible? If the contemplation and investigation of the laws of matter as manifested in the material world, in their almost endless combinations and operations, be a proper field for scientific inquiry, does not sound philosophy demand that the Bible shall be permitted to pour its superior light upon the pathway of scientific explorations, by lifting the mind to the great central power and originator of every law and property of matter? There is not a single scientific fact but what sustains a relation to a high and heavenly source, that the word of God alone reveals.

But a still higher scientific consideration for the general use of the Bible, and consequently its retention in our public schools, is found in the fact, as we have already seen, that it alone reveals that higher philosophic system of moral relations and obligations that relate to our race, both as it respects the life that now is, and that which is to come. Nothing can possibly be of greater importance to mankind than reliable information upon these momentous subjects. Man may carry his investigations down deep in the great laboratory of nature, or into the immeasurable regions of space, until he is astonished at the results of his attainments and the magnificence of the scenes that surround him; and yet without a knowledge of his own origin, nature, relations, obligations, duties, accountability, and the final destiny that awaits him, his round of information would be but half completed. Where else except in this blessed book shall we learn of that better land that no mortal eye hath yet seen—the heavenly Jerusalem, the metropolis of the universe, where Jehovah dwells in unsullied splendor? Where else shall we learn of angels, those superior intelligent beings, who surround His throne and do His pleasure, and who are employed to minister to our spiritual welfare: "Are they not all ministering spirits, sent forth to minister to them who shall be heirs of salvation?"

The Bible is absolutely indispensable as a literary work. Dr. Todd has justly said:

"It is found that in no other book is the power of reading so quickly acquired; and as to the *intellect*, the man aiming at high attainments as a lawyer, who is to deal with a jury, must be a reader of the Bible.

"John Marshall, the very prince of chief-justices, was a very Apollos in the Scriptures. He who created the light for the eye, and the sound for the ear, and the sandy desert for the camel's foot, created that book for the human intellect. It is the first book ever written on the earth, and doubtless will be the last book read; the eldest daughter of time, and so wise that all created minds cannot find a substitute. It is read by more readers, and in more languages, than any and all other books. Can you point to any other book which is printed and read in one hundred and seventy different languages? and of which one drops from the press once in four minutes the year round?

"For two hundred and fifty years the Bible

has been read in our schools, and generally through the land. I have yet to hear the first instance in which it has been injurious to the intellect or to the heart; on the contrary, you can point to no people, of the same numbers, having equal responsibilities laid upon them, who have developed so much intelligence, so much character, so much energy, and who have done so much for humanity, as these people who have grown up in our free schools, having read the Bible every day of their school-life.

"For good or for evil, read by young and old, the Bible has hitherto had a mighty influence in shaping the destiny of this nation. Nowhere on earth has it been read more, and nowhere under its teachings have risen up better schools, freer churches, better teachers, stronger men in the professions, nobler models in the halls of legislation and the senate."

In view of these facts, the absolute and indisputable superiority of the Bible over all other books, how truly astonishing are the efforts of Papists and others to expel this blessed book from our public schools! How strange the attempt to close up to our children one of the avenues to a knowledge of the Word of life, God's revelation to man! If no one, of all these objectors to its use in our schools, can point out a single instance in which any person, old or young, in school or out of school, was ever injured by it in any way, while on the other hand the most elevated in sentiment, benevolent in purpose, pure in thought, exemplary in life, and strong in the right, in all ages, whether old or young, have been those who have read and loved the Bible most, how strange the infatuation and madness, to say nothing of the wickedness, that seeks to expel the Bible from our schools, as though it would corrupt rather than purify!

CHAPTER XII.

Our Public Schools are not made Sectarian by the use of the Bible, as charged by Romanists.

ONE of the charges brought by Roman Catholics against our public schools, and urged by them as a reason why they should be broken up, is that they are made sectarian by the reading of the Holy Scriptures to the children. This is certainly a serious charge, and demands an investigation. As much as we believe in the necessity of the inculcation of great moral truths in our common schools, so as to impress the minds of the young, we are not willing that morality shall be taught in them according to the shiboleth of any sect or denominational creed. However valuable creeds and forms may be as bonds of union among the various denominations, they can never be admitted into our common schools, supported by the public funds of the State. This, indeed, would be just grounds for dissatisfaction and denunciation. The very nature of our government forbids it.

But is it true, as alleged by Romanists, that our public school system is justly liable to so serious an allegation? We most unhesitatingly and unqualifiedly answer no! Never was there a charge more groundless. It is the sheerest nonsense to affirm that the Bible, read in our schools without note or comment, makes them sectarian. As well affirm that to inculcate justice and virtue, is to inculcate sectarianism. The Bible is not a sectarian book in any sense. It was given for the benefit of all without regard to sect, race, or color.

If to read the Bible without note or comment is to be sectarian, and if to read it thus in our common schools is to sectarianize them, then for the State to enforce the observance of the Sabbath, is also sectarianism; to open our halls of legislation with the solemnities of religious worship, according to this theory, is to convert them into sectarian assemblies; to admit the Bible into courts of justice according to this plea is to make them sectarian courts. "In the courts over which we preside," says Judge O'Neall, "we daily acknowledge Christianity as the most solemn part of our administration. A Christian witness having no religious scruples against placing his hand upon the book, is sworn upon the holy Evangelists, the books of the New Testament, which testify of our Saviour's birth, life, death, and resurrection. This is so common a matter, that it is little thought of as affording any evidence of the part which Christianity has in the common law." But according to the charge brought against our public schools, these courts are sectarian courts, and made so by the use of the Bible. The Bible a sectarian book! As well might it be affirmed that Christianity itself is a sectarian institution —that the Lord Jesus Christ, together with the Apostles, were the originators and inculcators of sectarianism, and that Jehovah is a sectarian God. The Bible is the common property of mankind; the great and primary fountain of wisdom, righteousness, and truth; the supreme and unerring rule for the faith and practice of all men. How can it therefore be regarded in any sense as sectarian? or how can its being read in our schools without note or comment give them a sectarian bias?

But it is sometimes charged by Romanists that our Bible is made sectarian by its translation. Now, is it true, as claimed by them, that King James's translation of the Bible, which is used in our schools, is sectarian, or that it is a Protestant Bible, and consequently unreliable? In other words, is our English Bible, which we have been taught from childhood to love and cherish as the word of God, a sectarian book? Was it translated by men whose minds were so warped by prejudice against Romanism, and in favor of Protestantism, as to unfit them for an impartial rendering of the sense of the original? Such are the charges of Romanists.

But what are the facts in the case? Why, so far is this from being true, that it is a matter of history, that to a great extent it is a translation of Roman Catholics themselves. Wickliff, Tyndale, Coverdale, and Matthew, whose translations furnish the type and pattern of our English Bible, were all Roman Catholics. Bishop Leddes, also a Romanist, says of our English Bible : "*It is of all versions the most excellent for accuracy, fidelity, and the strictest letter of the text.*" Says the learned Selden : " It is the best version in the world." " If accuracy, fidelity and strict attention to the text," says Dr. Geddes, " be supposed to constitute the qualities of an excellent version, this, of all versions, must in general be accounted the most excellent. Every sentence, every word, every syllable, every letter and every point, seem to have been weighed with the most exactitude, and expressed either in the text or in the margin with the greatest precision."

Professor Taylor Lewis has well said :

"The reason of so little actual diversity in modern translations comes from the fact, that they were made by *scholars in the face of scholars*, who would immediately detect anything like forgery, interpolation, or the least departure from the substantial, and readily ascertainable text and grammatical sense of the original writings. Ignorant Romanists may make such a charge of falsifying; it may be connived at by reckless Jesuits; but no truly learned Catholic would venture the assertion, or dare to accept a challenge in such a controversy. Men like Dupanloup and Montalembert know better; the learned Catholics of Germany would never think of facing their learned Protestant compeers on such wholly untenable ground. Infidelity here may bluster, as it has always done: it may call to its aid the ignorance, or superficiality, of an unbiblical literary world; but the fact remains--the wonderful preservation, the wonderful unity and agreement of our written Scriptures amid all outward diversities of form, and all changes of language. What would we think if we heard men talk of a Protestant Homer, and a Catholic Homer, a French Homer, a German Homer, an English Homer, with allusion to translations of the old Greek poem into these respective languages? And yet it could be better justified than anything of the kind in respect to the Holy Scriptures."

Again, speaking of such men as Pascal and Fenelon, who loved the word of God for the sake of the truth, he further says:

"But men like these, we may well believe, would never think of stigmatizing the version of King James, or that of Luther, as a false heretical book, to be classed among profane and infidel productions, and to be read only on peril of damnation. Although Rome has long been opposed to the reading of the Scriptures by the common people, even when accessible in Catholic translations, yet it is only in modern times that such a style of speaking has been employed by her towards versions known to have come from the highest scholarship of the Reformation. It has been because since that period there has come a new thing into Rome itself, a new plague, exceeding in evil that of the former papacy, dark as was its mediæval history. When, therefore, we say Rome, we mean Rome strictly—Papal Rome, *Jesuit Rome*, Rome 'that sitteth on the seven hills'—and not that great and venerable body called 'the Catholic Church' as it exists in Europe, and on which this Papal power has so long been sitting like a dire, stifling incubus she could not throw off.

* * * * * * *

"The Jesuit opposition to the Bible in our schools, is an opposition to the Bible itself, to any Bible, to any version, under whatever form it may come, and from whatever authority it may emanate. For centuries has Rome been seeking to get wholly off from the platform of the Scriptures, and to seat herself broadly and firmly upon another—even the foundation of absolute Papal infallibility. There can be no compromise with her. The Jesuit is dishonest in this matter, and the Protestant who is aiding him by making our schools as irreligious as he describes them, is, to say the least, unwise. Courtesy may prevent our calling him 'foolish,' but we cannot help regarding his course as being most mischievous, as it is most inexcusable."

Dr. Clark says:

"Those who have compared most of the European translations with the original, have not scrupled to say that the English translation of the Bible, made under King James I., is the most accurate and faithful of the whole."

The charge that the Protestant Bible is a sectarian Bible, and consequently unfit, on that account, to be used in our public schools, comes with an ill grace from Roman Catholics, who have never published, or permitted their people to read any other than a purely sectarian Roman Catholic Bible. Even the Douay version has the decision of Councils and Papal notes appended to various passages in the form of comments and explanations, that renders it emphatically a sectarian Bible. For the purpose of sanctioning and sustaining the peculiar characteristics and sectarian dogmas of their Church, in the face of opposing texts, many of these appended notes so change, prevert, or neutralize these passages which they profess to explain, as to make them speak a language altogether foreign to the meaning of the Divine mind. Thus in the note on Ex. xx : 4, "Thou shalt not make unto thee any graven image," etc. It is said that "images, pictures, or representations even in the house of God, and in the very sanctuary, so far from being forbidden, are expressly authorized by the word of God."* Certainly no one but a Romanist would ever imagine the least possible harmony between the sacred text and the explanation.

Again: on Matthew xxvi., 26, "This is my body," etc., the note appended says: "He does not say this is the *figure* of my body, but this is my body. Neither does he say *in* this or *with* this is my body: which plainly implies transubstantiation." But how can this interpre-

* 2 Council of Nice, Act 6.

tation possibly be correct? It is positively absurd to suppose while Christ was still living that he held his own body (dead) between his own thumb and fingers. This forced interpretation to bolster up a purely sectarian dogma, if carried out would make the phrase "This cup is the new testament," etc., to mean that the material vessel, (not the wine in it), was an actual "new testament" which everybody knows to be false. It would make the "three branches" in the Butler's dream that Joseph interpreted to be three literal days, instead of representing three days. It would make the seven animals that Pharaoh saw in his dream, seven *literal* years, instead of representing seven years, as they obviously did. So by this false principle of interpretation they make the bread in the sacrament to *be* the body of Christ instead of representing it.

To the words of our Lord, "Drink ye all of this," is added by way of explanation the following note: "It no ways follows from these words that all the faithful are commanded to drink of the chalice," etc. And so the Church of Rome disobeys this positive command of Christ by withholding the wine in the sacrament from the laity, and falls back on the false interpretation for authority for so doing.

On 1st Tim. ii., 5, "For there is one God and one Mediator," etc., we read: "The only

Mediator, who stands in need of no other to recommend his petitions to the Father. This is not against our seeking the prayers and intercessions * * of the *saints* and *angels*," etc. Here the express and unequivocal declaration of the Apostle is completely neutralized by the explanation. This would not be so bad of itself, were it not that these Papal notes are regarded by Papists as being equal in authority with the word of God. These notes, coupled with this fact, make the Douay version most emphatically a sectarian Bible, while King James's version, which is used in our schools, is entirely free from any such just charge.

But after all this outcry of Romanists against the use of our Bible in the schools, because, as they allege, it is a Protestant Bible, is the merest hypocrisy. This is evident from the fact that they are unwilling that their own version—the Douay Bible—about the only real sectarian Bible as we have seen, should be in the schools. The *Freeman's Journal,* that speaks understandingly upon this subject, says:

"If the Catholic translation of the books of Holy Writ, which is to be found in the homes of all our better educated Catholics, were to be dissected by the ablest Catholic theologians in the land, and merely *lessons* to be taken from it—such as Catholic mothers read to their children; and with all the notes and comments, in the popular edition, and others added, with the highest

Catholic endorsement—and if these admirable Bible lessons, and these alone, were to be *ruled* as to be read in all the public schools, this would not diminish, in any substantial degree, the objection we Catholics have to letting Catholic children attend the public schools."

This, and other declarations from authoritative sources, show, conclusively, that it is not a question of version; but a question of Bible or no Bible. The book itself must be kept away from the children. Romanists have always claimed that the Bible was "not a book to be in the hands of the people," much less to be in the hands of minors. The question of version is the merest pretext. They are opposed to any version and every version—to the Bible in any form. The complaint that our schools are sectarian, and made so by reading the Bible without interpretation or comment, is the sheerest nonsense. This foolish charge, if carried out to its legitimate results, would lie equally against many of our school *text-books* which quote the Bible, or enforce its rules of life. Our grammars would have to be revised, and not only Bible quotations in parsing lessons taken out, but all quotations from works commending Bible precepts. All histories, giving Bible facts, and dates, would have to be suppressed for the same reason. The result of all this is easily seen. Our schools would be ruined. And this is unquestionably the purpose of the Romanist.

They have no sympathy for them, nor interest in them. The common school system is the legitimate offspring of Protestantism. We have them because we are not under the dominion and control of Popery. Romanism is the avowed enemy of popular and general education. Her whole past history is a confirmation of her hostility to unsectarian institutions of learning. The period of the meridian of her power and glory was the period of the midnight of the world's history, known as the dark ages. It will not, therefore, do for us to suffer Romanists to destroy our educational institutions under any pretext whatever, or to dictate to us what are our duties in respect to this question. We as Protestants, and as Americans, are entrusted with responsibilities that must be cheerfully borne. We are threatened with dangers that must be boldly and promptly met, without fear or favor.

CHAPTER XIII.

Our Public School System is not subversive of the Rights of Romanists.

It is claimed by Romanists, that in consequence of the use of the Bible in our public schools, and the exclusion of dogmatic theology as taught by their Church, the schools are rendered offensive to all true Catholics, and that as they are taxed in common with others to support these schools, they are unjustly oppressed.

In view of these imaginary grievances, they have denounced our public school system in unmeasured terms of reprobation, and evince a resolute determination to secure their destruction. They have even gone so far in their hostility to these institutions of education as to council in many instances rebellion against the enforcement of the law that levies taxes upon them for their share of their support. "A Catholic Priest," in the Boston *Advertiser*, says: "They (the Catholics) *will not be taxed* either for educating the children of Protestants, or for having their own children educated in schools under Protestant control." The Roman Catholic press to a great extent, throughout the country, is equally positive and defiant in its utterances. "A *swindle* on the people, an *outrage* on *justice*," and such like epithets have been deemed by them as proper characteristics of our school system.

It is true that our public school system was not organized solely in the interest of Popery, and that it does not admit the inculcation of their sectarian theology. But it is equally true that it does not admit the inculcation of Calvinism, or Armenianism, or the peculiar tenets of any sect whatever. This fact constitutes one of its best features. On no other plan could it succeed at all. This cuts off all reasonable complaint, upon this score, from every quarter. That the rights of the Roman Catholics are not invaded by being taxed to support these schools or by the use of the Bible in them, is made evident by the following considerations:

First, Romanists stand precisely in the same relation to this question that all others sustain, so far as treatment is concerned. They are protected in their rights just as any other sect is protected. They are taxed to support public schools just as others are taxed. There is certainly no wrong done them in this. The plea that they are oppressed and wronged by being taxed to support schools in which they have no interest, does not change the case in the least. Many others are taxed for this purpose, while they have no personal interest in the matter. Perhaps there is not a single institution in the land that is supported by taxation, but what some would claim as oppressive, just to the extent that they were taxed for its support. Yet so long as they are treated in the matter just as others are treated, taxed just as others are taxed, they have no reason to complain.

Why should Romanists imagine that they were wronged as such, by being compelled to contribute their part to support the public school system in which they do not believe, any more than Quakers should think that they were wronged in being compelled to contribute their part toward supporting military establishments in which they do not believe? The latter do not demand that the government shall give up military establishments to please them. Neither should the former require that the State should give up free schools for their sake. The State deems both of these institutions as important to its welfare, and consequently has the undoubted right to tax both of these classes, as well as others, for their support.

Again: it is a principle that lies at the very foundation of all democratic governments, that minorities must yield to majorities. In no country has this principle been more fully recognized and acted upon than in this. Every State election as well as more general elections, imposes upon thousands the necessity of submitting to measures that they not only dislike, but which in some instances they utterly abhor, without a thought of ever resisting, or feeling that they are in the least wronged. Those who are not willing to submit to majorities had better leave this country.

It should be also remembered, that in the organization of society, individuals must necessarily give up certain individual rights for the good of the whole. All personal rights that would conflict with the rights of the community, must be surrendered for the public weal. No principle is better established than this. Civil society is a necessity to civilization, and whatever is necessary to its permanency and prosperity, it has the right to enact, demand, impose, and enforce upon all its members, be their religious convictions and theories what they may. The compensation for this is furnished by society, in the better protection and greater security given to the individual.

Hence, in many instances, the law of society seems to conflict with individual rights, as when a Jew is compelled to observe the first day of the week as the Sabbath, while his religion and his conscience compel him to keep the seventh also, by which his business suffers the loss of fifty-two days more in the year than the business of most of his neighbors. In the same way Atheists and all who disbelieve in the Scriptural doctrine of future rewards and punishments, are restricted in their civil rights, by being prohibited from exercising privileges that are accorded to others. So by the same law Quakers are shut out from all judicial offices, as their consciences will not allow them to administer oaths as required by law. The rule is, that no individual, or class of individuals, shall have the liberty to exercise even what he or they may please to call a right of conscience, when such exercise will tend to endanger the prosperity or welfare of the State. This rule gives to society the undoubted right to tax even Roman Catholics in connection with all others, for the maintenance of its public schools; and if the State has this right (which cannot be questioned), then the rights of Romanists are not invaded, nor are they wronged by the measure.

Dr. Wayland has justly said: "Society having adopted a particular form of government, they bind themselves to whatever is *necessary* to the existence of that government. Thus, if men choose a republican form of government, in which the people are acknowledged to be the fountain of all power, they come under the obligation to educate their children intellectually and morally; for, without intellectual and moral education, such a form of government cannot long exist. And, as the intellectual education of the young can be made properly a subject of social enactment, this duty may be *enforced* by society."*

Here it is affirmed not only that if the State deems public schools necessary to the promotion of intelligence in the nation, and the use of the Bible in those schools, for the development of a wholesome moral sentiment among the people in view of its own permanency, it has an undoubted right to establish them by a system of taxation, but that it is made the solemn *duty* of the State to do this very thing; and that such taxation must be held to be in harmony with the rights of individuals and sects, who may differ in their views with the law of the land.

But our Roman Catholic neighbors tell us that their " consciences are offended by this whole public school business, and that they cannot, and will not consent to be taxed for its support."

This plea of violated consciences on the part of papists is the merest pretense; a plea without a reason; especially when based, as it is, upon the reading of the Bible in the schools. Their consciences offended by their children being made acquainted with God's word; his glorious character; their relation to Him; their

* Wayland's Moral Science, p. 390.

duty and destiny! What an absurdity! Such a conscience is very much like those consciences that burned thousands at the stake for daring to read the Bible or thinking for themselves. Conscience is a very strange thing with some people; and if nothing is to be done that may chance to violate some one's conscience, then all progress is at an end.

But after all, where is the wrong that is done them? If they choose to take their children from the public schools and establish sectarian schools of their own, where they can teach them in their own way, they have a perfect right to do so.

There is no law to compel them to send their children to the public schools. They can do in this matter just as they please. How, then, is their consciences violated? What right is invaded? As well might they claim that their rights were subverted and their consciences violated, by being taxed to support the military establishment at West Point, where but few of them will ever send their children at all. Even were it true that their consciences are offended, this would not give them the right to break up our public school system, either by diverting a part of the public funds raised by taxation for their support, to sectarian purposes, or in any other way. Our common schools have been established by the State for its own welfare.

They are the sacred juvenile churches of liberty, and it is utterly impossible that the principles of right should demand of us to sacrifice them to satisfy the consciences of any. Nay, we should rather firmly resist opposition to our schools from any quarter, although it be made in behalf of conscience. This principle has been recognized and made the basis of judicial decisions by the highest courts in our land.

Says the Supreme Court of Maine:

"'*Salus populi suprema lex*' (the public safety is the supreme law), is a maxim of universal application, and when the liberty of conscience would interfere with the paramount rights of the public *it ought to be restrained.* Even Mr. Jefferson, than whom a more resolute champion of liberty never lived, claimed no indulgence for anything that is detrimental to society, though it springs from a religious belief, or no belief at all. His position is that civil government is instituted only for temporal objects, and that spiritual matters are legitimate subjects of civil cognizance no farther than they may stand in the way of these objects. As far as the interests of society are involved, its right to interfere on the principle of self-preservation is not disputed."

The attempt of Romanists to justify their hostility to our public school system on the score of conscience, should deceive no one. Any thing and every thing that will serve as a pretext for waging against our school system an unceasing warfare, is seized upon by them, and used to the greatest possible extent.

158 Our School System not Oppressive.

If, however, Romanists still insist that inasmuch as their consciences are injured in this matter, they must be heard, and their convictions must be respected; we would most respectfully suggest, that Protestants have consciences too. True, their consciences do not rest upon the bulls of popes, the decisions of councils, or the traditions of monks, but simply upon the word of God. Yet we think their convictions are as strong and as much entitled to respect as the consciences of Romanists. And surely no one doubts that the consciences of Protestants would be as sorely tried by the expulsion of the Bible from our common schools, as are the consciences of Papists by its retention.

And now let me ask is it right, is it reasonable that the consciences of 20,000,000 of Protestants, enlightened by divine truth, shall surrender to 7,000,000 of Romanists? Besides this clamor for the expulsion of the Bible comes not from the mass of Roman Catholics, but principally from the priests and bishops who constitute comparatively a very small number indeed.

But this plea of conscience, as we have seen, can never be admitted, from the fact that it would be absolutely impossible for the State to accommodate the consciences of all. If the thing were attempted, it would necessarily result in, not only the destruction of our public school system, but in the destruction of all our free institutions; for if we yield to the demand of Papists on the score of conscience, we must, to be consistent, yield also to the demand of Jews, and Infidels, and Athiests, and Pagans, for they tell us that they have consciences too. When the Romish hierarchy has secured the expulsion of the Bible from our schools, on the plea that the State has nothing to do with religion, the Chinese population may next protest against any reference being made in those schools by books or otherwise to the Christian religion, in any form, and according to this doctrine, we must submit to this demand also. Such a system of operation would necessarily end in ruin.

CHAPTER XIV.

Shall we consent to Banish the Bible from the Public Schools to please Romanists, or any other sect?

This question, which never should have arisen, at least in this country, but which has nevertheless been thrust upon us by the demands of Papists to expel the Bible from our common schools, must be fairly and squarely met. Its vital importance to the whole country demands an early and honest decision. What that decision should be it is not difficult to divine. What it will be is not so certain. To those who may be wavering in their minds upon this question, and to such as may be indifferent to the subject altogether, we would most respectfully submit the following considerations.

In the first place this nation is emphatically a Protestant nation. We believe in the Bible, and justly esteem it as a revelation from God. It has not only given us the elements out of which has been laid the foundation of our free institutions, but it has given us our religion and the liberty to worship God according to the dictates of our own consciences. As a people, we are under the most solemn obligations to circulate it among all mankind, to put it in the hands of all classes. And this obligation to make its contents known to every human being includes children as well as adults. It would be a singular interpretation of duty that would lead us to send the Bible to heathen lands and yet withhold it from our own children.

To Protestantism the Bible is the higher law, both in Church and State, in all the relations and duties of life. It is difficult to see how we can banish it from our public schools without being recreant to the sacred trust that has been committed to us by our fathers. Yet in the face of all these facts, we are seriously asked by Romanists, nay more, they demand that we shall banish the Bible from our schools because, as they affirm, it is an improper book for the young. That they should seek to withhold the Word of life from the children is not strange of itself, for they withhold it from the people; but that they should come here by our courtesy, and when, through the privileges we have extended to them, they have become a power among us, then to seek to change, overturn and break down our institutions, simply because there is no affinity between our free institutions and their Church, is truly astonishing. Was there ever an instance of greater arrogance and presumption? Look at the following facts. We have in the United States some 65,000 common schools, with about 7,000,000 of pupils, supported at an annual expense of about $8,000,000 —nine-tenths of which or more is paid by Protestants. Besides, we have a population of some 38,000,000. The highest number that Roman Catholics can claim with any show of reason, is about 7,000,000. Now, allowing that there are 3,000,000 of Infidels and Atheists who are also opposed to the Bible, and who with Romanists insist on its expulsion from our schools, we have 28,000,000 of Protestants who are required to surrender an important principle to the unreasonable demand of 7,000,000 of Romanists!

Now is this right, is it reasonable, or just? Where is the law, human or divine, that would require Protestants to give up a great principle in order to make way for the advancement of a sect that is governed by a foreign ruler, who is a perfect despot in practice as well as in theory, and who is an intense hater of republicanism in all its forms?

A Roman Catholic in lamenting the general use of the Bible as a strong barrier in the way of the success of Popery, has unwittingly presented some strong reasons why we as Protestants should continue it in our schools. He says: "Who will not say that the uncommon beauty and marvellous English of the Protestant Bible is one of the great strongholds of heresy in this

Shall we Banish the Bible? 163

country? It lives on the ear like music that can never be forgotten, like the sound of church bells, which the convert hardly knows how to forego. Its felicities often seem to be almost things rather than words. It is part of the national mind, and the anchor of national seriousness. The memory of the dead passes with it. The potent traditions of childhood are stereotyped in its verses. The power of all the griefs and trials of a man are hidden beneath its words. It is the representative of his best moments, and all that there has been about him of soft and gentle, and pure, and penitent, and good, speaks to him forever out of his English Bible. It is his sacred thing, which doubt has never dimmed, and controversy never soiled. In the length and breadth of the land there is not a Protestant with one spark of religiousness about him, whose spiritual biography is not in his Saxon Bible."

Now if it be a fact, as is here stated even by a Romanist, and as it seems to me must be admitted by all, namely, that the Bible is "the anchor of national seriousness," that it is the representative of man's best moments, and all there has been about him of soft and gentle, and pure, and penitent, and good, speaks to him forever out of his English Bible, why not have it in our schools for the benefit of our children? Surely a book with such a character and such a record, and such heavenly influences, must prove a great blessing to them as well as to adults.

There is another thought in this connection, namely, if we banish the Bible from our public institutions of learning, then, to be consistent, we must banish it from all our State institutions. For if the Bible must be expelled from our public schools on the ground that they are supported by the State, and that the State has nothing to do with religion, or the moral education of the children, then on the same principle it must be excluded from every institution supported by the State. This is the inevitable logic of the premise claimed.

Now I ask, are we prepared to adopt a policy that will legitimately lead to this? Are we as Protestants ready to expel the Bible from the asylums of the blind, the deaf and dumb, from alms-houses, from the State schools established for the children of paupers and for juvenile offenders? In the schools connected with alms-houses, and in reformatory schools, are thousands of children, who, but for the reading of the Bible in these schools would, in all probability, never hear its sacred truths at all. Here is found, and perhaps here only, the opportunity of these poor outcasts, neglected as they are by vicious and criminal parents, who care not for the welfare of their souls, to learn the way of salvation. Shall this only avenue to religious knowledge now open to them, be cruelly closed against them to satisfy the unreasonable demands of Papists or any other class? Shall it be also excluded from our prisons? For these are also supported by the State; and the same reason that would exclude it from our juvenile institutions, would exclude it from our jails, prisons, and penitentiaries. This would be a severe blow to the benevolent operations and efforts of American philanthropists who have been toiling for the last fifty years to improve our prison discipline, so as to reform our criminals, and prevent their return to criminal practices. But how can this be done without the use of the Bible?

General Pilsbury, Superintendent of the Albany Penitentiary, says in his report: "We have a copy (of the Bible) in every cell, and the prisoners read it through several times. They often express to me their deep interest in its narratives and truths, and some have said they found something new in the Bible every time they read it. Several have committed whole chapters to memory, and the men who do the most work in the shops of the prisons are those who learn most of the Bible." Now shall we voluntarily enter upon a pathway that inevitably leads to the banishment of the Word of life from our prisons, and thereby make them resemble the prisons of Spain and Italy, in the cells of which the Bible is never found? Shall we, in a word, make them resemble the prisons of heathen lands, by withholding from our criminals the book that can above all others reach their hearts, enlighten their minds, and cheer their souls by directing them to the "Lamb of God that taketh away the sins of the world"? Or who with one spark of humanity in his soul, would take from the blind asylums the sacred Scriptures, and thereby wickedly add to the terrible darkness that surrounds the blind, the deeper moral darkness that must follow their ignorance of God's revelation to man? Shall we do all this in order to put a stop to this controversy, and satisfy our Roman Catholic neighbors? Some say yes! we had better do all this to satisfy them and thus save our schools. But can we not save our schools and the Bible too? Will we be stronger by surrendering a strong position to the enemy, and that the very key to our encampment—the citadel itself? Can we make a more vigorous stand for our public school system, when tens of thousands of its friends are alienated and disheartened by the expulsion of the Bible therefrom?

Besides, where is the evidence that these concessions will satisfy the Catholics, or end the controversy, or save our schools? They demand that our public schools shall be purely irreligious, or in other words secular, so that the higher ideas of morality shall be entirely excluded. Now is it not manifest that other books would soon be required to be placed under ban for inculcating the moral truths of the Bible? No such reading book could be allowed according to this absurd theory of Romanists, that every thing religious must be excluded.

The *Catholic World*, a leading paper of that denomination, in an issue of July last, in an article entitled "The Catholics of the Nineteenth Century," says:

"The supremacy asserted for the church in matters of education implies the additional and cognate function of the censorship of ideas, and the right to examine and approve or disapprove all books, publications, writings and utterances intended for public instruction, enlightenment or entertainment."

So it is not the Bible only over which they propose to exercise supervision, but "*all books.*" If we give up the Bible because it is offensive to them, how can we retain any book that they may see proper to condemn? The reasons that would be sufficient in the one case would be equally so in the other. If they may dictate to us in reference to our Bible, why not in reference to any other book?

Now who does not see that to allow such an interference, such a censorship over our public schools, would not only belittle ourselves, but prove absolutely ruinous to the whole system? Let this but be followed out to its logical results, and it would exclude some of the most important branches of literature from our educational institutions. The sciences of life and motion, physiology and chemistry, rise above the secular. The same is true of a great part of history, geology, psychology, philosophy, ethics, and astronomy. They can never be confined to such narrow and unnatural limitations. The whole theory, that our public schools should be secular only, is perfectly absurd, and can never be tolerated without securing their destruction.

But perhaps it may be said that the Catholics will never interfere with any of our schoolbooks except the Bible, that with its expulsion they will be satisfied, and that our schools will then be out of danger. Now granting this to be the case, (which is perfectly absurd,) would it not be better that our public school system run the risk of being ruined (through Catholic hostility,) by doing right, by holding on to the Bible, than to secure apparent stability by doing wrong? Would it not be better for our schools to suffer Papal hostility rather than our children be deprived of moral instruction? Can we yield to this demand to expel the Bible from our schools, on the principles of honesty, integrity and virtue; and by so doing give up the very basis of our national life? While we are sending the Bible to other lands, shall we consent to close the doors of 65,000 schools against it at home? Shall it be said that 28,000,000 of Protestants surrendered, without a struggle, Protestant principles, and the Bible in the bargain, to the demand of some 7,000,000 of Bible haters and Bible burners? That our reverence for Popery was so profound, that we willingly sacrificed our public schools, the Bible and our country too, to help the Pope to establish his supremacy in the United States, that he might tread our institutions in the dust, and give us in exchange for our boasted system of religious toleration, the inquisition? That, like craven sycophants, in our attempt to secure the friendship of Rome, we sacrificed the friendship of God? Let Protestants answer!

Let it be also remembered that it is not a question as to whether the Bible shall be introduced into our schools, but whether or not it shall be banished therefrom. A very different element, not only in kind but in degree, is contained in the latter as compared with the former. The question of admission involves a matter of mere expediency, that of expulsion an act of hostility. The former expresses no opinion on its character, the latter puts it under ban by an official interdiction as pernicious and hurtful. Such a course would at once place us alongside of Papists, Infidels and Atheists, by which in this particular we would act like them and with them. Should we voluntarily surrender to the demands of Rome, and expel the Bible from all our public institutions of learning, how could we at any future time remonstrate with Popery for withholding the Scriptures from the people? Would she not quickly, in such an event, point us to our own act in placing them upon the list of proscribed books, at least so far as public schools were concerned? After such a consummation, how completely would we be overwhelmed with confusion, to see one of our own strongholds not only in the hands of a triumphant foe, but its guns turned upon our retreating, decimated and broken columns?

CHAPTER XV.

Why Romanists are Opposed to the Bible.

NOTWITHSTANDING the Lord Jesus has commanded us, in the most explicit manner, to *search the Scriptures,* the Romish hierarchs, as we have seen, have declared in language equally as explicit, "you shall not search the Scriptures, nor read them without our permission." And all the power and influence Rome possesses are employed to prevent their free circulation among the people; and as we have also seen, this prohibition extends to Romish as well as to Protestant translations.

Now the question naturally arises, Why are the Romish hierarchs opposed to the Bible? Why do they interdict its circulation, as though it were pernicious to good morals, and unfit for vulgar eyes? The Apostle Peter, who is claimed by Romanists to have been the first Pope, seems to have entertained very different views upon this subject. In speaking of the "cunningly devised fables" of his day, as unreliable and sophistical, he refers to the Scriptures as "a more sure word of prophecy; *whereunto,*" says he, "*ye do well that ye take heed, as unto a light that shineth in a dark place.*" Here Peter calls the Scriptures a light, and exhorts *all* believers to make themselves acquainted with them. We are also informed by the historian that in keeping with this exhortation, "in the early ages of the Church its universal perusal was not only allowed but urged by bishops and pastors."

Why then is it that for hundreds of years past the Popes and bishops of Rome have pursued a course so directly opposite to this? The answer is furnished in the teachings of Christ. "Every one that doeth *evil* hateth the *light*, neither *cometh to* the *light*, lest his *deeds* should be *reproved*. But he that doeth *truth* cometh to the *light*, that his deeds may be made *manifest* that they are wrought of *God*." Here is a solution of the whole matter. The Church of Rome having departed from the truth naturally arrays herself against it. "Every one" that doeth evil hateth the light, and Rome is not an exception to this rule. This divergency of the Romish Church from the teachings of the Scriptures, which was small in the beginning, became very manifest in the sixth century. The Popes, in order to increase their authority and extend their dominion, gave the preference to human compositions above the Scriptures. As the Bible did not favor the ambitious projects of the Pope, it gradually fell into disrepute, while the opinions of doctors and decisions of Councils were regarded as better authority than the word of God. In this way it soon became a dead letter. To further the unscriptural designs of the Papacy, forged papers were produced from time to time to sanction some further innovation upon primitive usages. Among these documents were the famous *decretal epistles*, said to have been written by former pontiffs, that were now brought forward with great triumph. Having turned their backs upon the Bible, and substituted human authority in its stead, it was not so strange that they should go to the heathens to borrow their Pagan rites and senseless mummeries. This (to her shame be it spoken) she did to an extent that has left thousands at a loss to determine whether she is more Christian or Pagan.

One of these prominent Pagan rites that has been unqualifiedly condemned by the word of God, viz. : image worship, was gradually introduced, but did not become the law of the Church until 786, when by the second council of Nice, "the *worship of images*, and of the *cross* was established, and *penalties* were denounced against those who should maintain that *worship and adoration were to be given only to God*."* Thus at this early period the odious system of idolatry was incorporated into the Papal system, and established by the

* Moshiem's Ec. His., v. ii., p. 41.

highest authority of that Church. Is it, therefore, any wonder that Rome should hate the book that reprovingly says: "*Thou shalt not make unto thee any graven image, or any likeness of any thing that is in heaven above, or that is in the earth beneath, or that is in the water under the earth: Thou shalt not bow down thyself to them,*" etc. Most assuredly not.

This command forbids even the worship of the true God by or through images. The Jews so understood it, and thought themselves forbidden by this commandment to make any image or picture whatever, or to countenance them in any way in connection with their religious worship. Hence the images which the Roman armies had in their ensigns were called an abomination to them, especially when set up in the holy place.

This command positively forbids making any image of God, or the "likeness of *any thing that is in heaven above,* or that is on the earth beneath," etc. And consequently they were forbidden to have any image before them for so much as exciting, directing, or assisting their devotions, and for this plain and palpable reason, that if they bowed down before images, whatever might be the pretext, they would be doing just as idolaters did around them. The Apostle says of the heathens that they "changed the glory of the incorruptible God into an image like to corruptible man," etc., and that in doing so they "changed the truth of God into a lie," by teaching by the help of images that God has a body and parts as man has, and that he is material, whereas the word tells us that "God is a spirit," and consequently cannot be represented by any image whatever. This command also expressly forbids our having the image or likeness of any thing on earth or under the earth, connected with our devotions.

It is sometimes denied by Roman Catholics that they worship images, and that in this respect they are like the heathens. But the Council of Trent, the highest authority in the Roman Catholic Church, says, in speaking of the duty of bishops: "Let them teach that the images of Christ, of the Virgin Mother of God, and of other Saints, are to be had and retained, especially in the churches, and due honor and veneration rendered to them." Even the Doway Bible, in a note on Ex. xx., 4, says: "images, pictures and representations, even in the house of God, and in the very sanctuary, so far from being forbidden, are expressly authorized by the word of God." But where in the word of God? Where, save in the Creed and teachings of the Roman Catholic Church as declared by her councils; for the Bible, as we have seen, most expressly forbids it. This fact is plainly felt by Romanists, and they have accordingly adopted various expedients to get rid of the difficulty; one of which is to leave out this command altogether, joining the reason of it to the first; and so calling the third the second, and so on to the last, which they divide into two, to make up the number ten. This plan has been adopted, I am told, in all their catechisms and books of devotion, which are designed for the common people, lest they should become too familiar with the glaring discrepancy that exists between the word of God and the teachings and practices of their church. Everybody knows that the universal practice of Papists is to bow before and adore the images and pictures that adorn the walls of their churches, in all lands, according to the instruction of the Council of Trent. True, Romanists tell us that they do not worship the images themselves, but rather the person or persons that the images represent. The Council of Trent also says: "The honor with which they (the images) are regarded is referred to those who are represented by them; so that we adore Christ and venerate the saints, whose likenesses these images bear, when we kiss them, and uncover our heads in their presence, and prostrate ourselves." But this is precisely the way that educated heathens tell us that they worship their idols; that they do not worship the material statue or picture, but that which they represent; and just as Roman Catholics justify their image worship, so do heathens, by the same kind of reasoning, justify their whole system of idolatry. No well-informed Greek or Roman believed that the images in the Parthenon at Athens, or the Pantheon at Rome, were the real gods and goddesses, but merely the images or representations of their real divinities.

A native of India who was some time since in London, said in justification of their system of idolatry, as quoted by Dr. Mattison: "We have in our temples an image of Deity to look at, with large eyes, huge ears, great hands, and long feet. Not that we believe the very image to be the Deity, but we use it only to fix our attention, and to remind us that the being which it represents can see everything, hear everything," etc. Thus it is seen that Roman Catholics have images for the same purpose that heathens do, and worship them in the same manner precisely that heathens worship theirs; and that they both justify their idolatry in the same manner; so that, in this respect, they both stand on the same footing. No one therefore can pretend, with the least show of reason, that the whole system of Roman Catholic image worship differs in any material respect from heathen idolatry which is found in China, Japan, India, and all other heathen lands to this day. Whatever Pagans do to their images,

Roman Catholics do to theirs; for, as Jeremy Taylor says : " They consecrate them; they hope in them; they expect gifts and graces from them; they clothe and crown them; they erect altars and temples to them; they kiss them; they bow their head and knee before them; they light up tapers and lamps to them, *which is a direct consumptive sacrifice;* they do to their images as heathens do to theirs," etc.

Is it any wonder that the Romish heirarchy who uphold and justify all'this abominable system of baptized idolatry, should seek to blot out the second command of the Decalogue, which so positively and unqualifiedly forbids the making and bowing to images; or to prohibit the circulation of the Scriptures among the people lest they should learn to distrust the professed infallibility of the church in its teachings? Thomas Linacer, a learned and celebrated Roman Catholic ecclesiastic, having never read the New Testament in his life, in his latter days undertook to do so, but he soon threw the volume aside, exclaiming with an oath, that, " Either this is not the *Gospel*, or else we (Roman Catholics) *are not Christians.*"*

This astonishing ignorance of the word of life in this dignatary of the Romish Church is not a solitary case by any means. Many such instances are well authenticated, that go to establish

*D'Aubigne His. of Ref., v. i., p. 67.

the fact beyond controversy, that the Bible, having fallen into disrepute because of its antagonism to Popery, was well nigh universally neglected and discarded by its priests and bishops. In no other way can we account for the above decision. While, however, his conclusion was a necessary one, unavoidable from the premises, his course of action was most unreasonable and reprehensible. He madly threw away the only infallible standard of faith and practice, to cling to a church whose customs, teachings and spirit were so glaringly at variance with its sacred precepts and doctrines, as to make it absolutely impossible to reconcile the one with the other. And it is plainly evident that Romanists are generally pursuing the same course to-day; honoring the church and her rites and ceremonies at the expense of the sacred Scriptures.

CHAPTER XVI.

The Paganism of Popery—The Celibacy of the Clergy Unscriptural and Pagan.

AMONG the various anti-scriptural dogmas and practices of the Romish Church that may be directly traced to Pagan asceticism (the fruitful source of many of her abominations,) is that of the prohibition of her priests to marry under pain of excommunication. The more is the enforcement of this anti-christian tenent to be deplored, as it has largely contributed to the profligacy and libertinism of many of her clergy, to the great scandal of religion. Just previous to the commencement of the Reformation, and during the dark ages—the noon-day of Popery —the licentiousness of most of the priests, bishops, and even Popes, is well nigh incredible. "*All the clergy,*" says an historian, "*kept mistresses, and all the convents of the capital were houses of ill fame.*"* Another writer says: "The abodes of the clergy were dens of corruption." D'Aubigne quotes from an author of those times the following: "What humiliating scenes did the house of a pastor present! The wretched man supported the woman and the

*D'Aubigne's His. of Ref., v. i., p. 64.

children she had borne him with the tithes and offerings. His conscience was troubled. He blushed in the presence of the people, before his domestics, and before God. The mother, fearing to come to want if the priest should die, made provision against it beforehand, and robbed her own house. Her honor was lost. Her children were ever a living accusation against her. Despised by all, they plunged into quarrels and debauchery. Such was the family of a priest.* Eramus is quoted as saying: "In many places the priest paid the bishop a regular tax for the woman with whom he lived, and for each child he had by her. A German bishop said publicly one day, at a great entertainment, that *in one year eleven thousand priests had presented themselves before him for that purpose.*"† Another writer says: "In many places the people were delighted at seeing a priest keep a mistress, *that the married women might be safe from his seductions.*" It is a well known fact that Rodrigo Borgia, who, having secured his elevation to the Popedom by the most unprincipled acts of bribery, and who is known as Pope Alexander VI., not only had his concubines, three of whom were a Roman lady and her two daughters, but who squandered the treasure of the Church to enrich his bastard children, and finally died a murderer.‡ Nor

* His. Ref., Vol. 1, p. 62. † Ibid, p. 63.
‡ See Bib. Theol. Ec. Cyc., Vol. 1, p. 145.

are these deplorable practices confined to former ages.

The same causes continue to lead to the same scandalous results. Evidences of this are not wanting, especially in Roman Catholic countries, where the restraining and purifying influences of Protestantism are unfelt and unknown. The more absolute and undisturbed the Papal system, the deeper the ecclesiastical corruption.

Our late Consul at Rome, W. J. Stillman, who resided there four years and who had ample opportunities for observation, and who, consequently, is well qualified to testify on this subject, after speaking of various other abuses and gross immoralities, says:

"Worse than this---worse than anything we can conceive—was the system of debauchery kept up by the priesthood. It was a proverb among the Romans that, 'if one would go to a house of *ill-fame* he must go by day, at night the *priests* had all the places,' and another, that, 'all married women were *seduced by the priests.*' The amours and profligacy of Antonelli were as well known as that of the late Emperor of France, and no one who has lived in Rome long can be unaware that the immorality of that city (except among the obstinate Liberals who rejected all prerogatives of the Church, as such) was [greater than any city in Europe, except Vienna and Naples, and worse in its type than that of the latter city."

Now where did Rome obtain this idea of

celibacy that has contributed so largely to the licentiousness of her priests and bishops? Surely, not from the word of God. Celibacy is nowhere enjoined on man or woman, saint or sinner, in the Old or New Testament. Under the Mosaic law priests were not only allowed, but encouraged to marry. Nay, it was made their duty by the laws of priesthood. There is nothing in the New Testament that even countenances enforced celibacy on any one. Peter, who is claimed by the Romanists to have been the first Pope, was certainly a married man. (Matt. viii: 14.) Philip, one of the seven deacons, was also a married man (Acts xxi: 9); and if our Lord did not require celibacy in the first preachers of the Gospel, he certainly does not now. Besides, Paul says: "*Let every man have his own wife.*" *Every man*, not even excepting ministers. Again he says, "Marriage is honorable in *all*." Here again there are no exceptions. When Aquila traveled about to preach the Gospel, he was not only married, but his wife Priscilla accompanied him (Acts xviii: 2).

True, a voluntary unmarried life was advised in the New Testament under certain peculiar circumstances, but it had no more to do with pastors than laymen; besides, there was no compulsion in any case. Paul, who was himself single, asserts his own right to marry, inasmuch as he claims the privilege of "carrying about a sister or a *wife*," as well as the other Apostles." (1 Cor. ix: 4.) In fact, it is very evident that Paul believed that as a rule pastors should marry, for he expressly says that "a *bishop* must be the husband of one *wife*." (1 Tim. iii: 3.) Moreover, the Apostle in describing the great apostacy that should follow, says: "Now the Spirit speaketh expressly, that in the latter times some should depart from the faith, giving heed to seducing spirits and doctrines of devils: speaking lies in hypocrisy; having their conscience seared with a hot iron; *forbidding to marry*," &c. (1 Tim. iv: 1–3.)

Here the Apostle, so far from making celibacy a positive precept for Christians, declares it to be a distinctive mark of apostacy. Consequently, for the first three hundred years, there was no enforced celibacy of the clergy, or any one else. Hence we read that Valens, presbyter of Philippe, had a wife; Cheremon, bishop of Nilus; Novatus, presbyter of Carthage; Cyprian, bishop of Carthage also, and Tertulian, a presbyter, all had wives.

But, notwithstanding the plain teachings of the Apostles on this subject, the opinion gradually gained ground that celibacy ought to be observed, until it was finally enforced by Pope Gregory VII., so that all married priests were compelled to abandon their wives or suffer excommunication. The ancient Pagan notion of a dualistic idea of good and evil principles, and that evil had its seat and existence in matter, began to be encouraged even in the third century. As the philosophy of Pythagoras and Plato began to be admired, Pagan customs began to be adopted. Among these was that of celibacy. This was its true origin—a heathen custom, nothing more. We find it in heathen mythology. The goddess Diana, who was worshiped by the ancient Greeks and the inhabitants of Asia Minor, was not only believed to have devoted herself to perpetual *celibacy*, but that she also had for her attendants eighty nymphs, who likewise abjured the institution of marriage. Their goddess Vesta also, who was held in such high esteem as to receive the first oblations in sacrifice, was worshiped as a *virgin*.

It is well known that the ancient Romans, who received many of their religious views from the Grecians, also held the same ascetic notions from which the idea of celibacy originated. According to Plutarch, Numa, who had much to do with regulating their Pagan rites, ceremonies, &c., not only built a temple to Vesta, but established the order of the Vestal Virgins, who were required to observe the vows of *celibacy* during the thirty years of their temple service, under the threatened penalty of a most terrible death in case of transgression.*

* Plutarch, Vol. 1, p. 240.

Hildebrand, who saw that this Pagan notion of celibacy, if adopted, would not only narrow down the difference between Popery and heathendom and thereby exalt the Church in the estimation of the latter, but would also contribute largely to the power of the Popes, by thus sundering every social tie of the priesthood, and in this way make them more efficient as his instruments, made it the law of the Church, in the face of the plainest teachings of the Scriptures to the contrary. The Church of Rome having thus ignored the word of God in this matter, and gone to heathens for counsel, and having proved themselves to have apostatized from the faith as foretold by the Apostle Paul, (1 Tim. iv.: 1–3.) by "*giving* heed to seducing spirits and doctrines of devils, *forbidding to marry*," &c., is there any wonder that they should have sought to keep the Bible in its pure and unadulterated state from the people, and to drive it out of our public schools? Paul says a bishop " must be the *husband* of one *wife*, having his *children* in subjection, for if a man know not how to rule his own house, (*i. e.*, *family*,) how shall he take care of the church of God," but Romanists say he shall have no wife. Thus they say one thing and the Bible says another. Between the two there is therefore an irrepressible conflict.

CHAPTER XVII.

The Paganism of Rome, the Secret of her Opposition to the Bible.

THE opposition of Rome to the circulation of the Scriptures without note or comment among the people, can only be accounted for by taking into consideration the distinctly marked antagonism, in many respects, between the teachings of the Bible on the one hand, and the numerous Pagan rites and ceremonies of the Church of Rome on the other. As we have seen, her gross and universal worship of images, which is downright idolatry, cannot be justified on the score of reason or revelation. This and her constant use of holy water, being as they truly are, purely heathen forms of a blind superstition, not only mark her Pagan character, but also array her against the Bible.

This heathenish practice of Rome, namely, the use of *holy water* as a religious rite, was introduced into her ritualistic forms in the sixth century. This water, prepared by ridiculous ceremonies, seemingly too absurd to admit of rational inspection, will, as it is affirmed, drive away devils, cancel venial sins—impart strength to resist temptation—dissipate wicked thoughts

—preserve from sickness—obtain the favor and presence of the Holy Ghost, etc.*

Hence the common practice among Papists to keep on hand a supply of *holy water* for almost constant use, in ways and on occasions too numerous to mention. In fact, to such a ridiculous extent is this absurd practice carried, that it is applied to animals as well as men. On St. Anthony's day in Rome, under the eye and patronage of the Pope, the deluded people of that city and the surrounding country bring their horses, mules and donkeys to the priests to be sprinkled with this *holy water*, to keep them, as they are taught by the priests, from injury, and in a healthy and thriving condition. But this by no means constitutes the sum of this ridiculous farce. If the application of holy water were confined to persons, there might be some excuse for the practice as a religious rite, or symbol. But in addition to horses, mules and donkeys, it is sprinkled upon houses, upon beds, upon meats, upon fortifications, upon cannon, upon bells, upon garments, upon coffins, upon candles, upon sheep, and dogs. "Nothing," says Croly, "can be blessed or hallowed without it. . . . . Even the butter churn is sprinkled with it before churning commences, that the cream may work the better. It purifies the air—heals distempers—cleanses the soul—

* See Apostolic Constitution.

expels Satan and his imps from haunted houses, and introduces the Holy Ghost as an inmate in their stead."

In the Church of S. Carlo Borromeo in the Corso at Rome, over the vessel of holy water is placed the following document for the information of the faithful :

" Holy water possesses much usefulness when Christians sprinkle themselves with it with due reverence and devotion. The Holy Church proposes it as a remedy and assistant in many circumstances both spiritual and corporeal, but especially in these following :

"ITS SPIRITUAL USEFULNESS.

" 1. It drives away devils from places and from persons.

" 2. It affords great assistance against fears and diabolical illusions.

" 3. It cancels venial sins.

" 4. It imparts strength to resist temptations and occasions to sin.

" 5. It drives away wicked thoughts.

" 6. It preserves safely from the passing snares of the devil, both internally and externally.

" 8. It obtains the favor and presence of the Holy Ghost, by which the soul is consoled, rejoiced, and excited to devotion and disposed to prayer.

" It prepares the human mind for a better attendance on the divine mysteries, and receiving piously and worthily the most holy sacrament.

"ITS CORPOREAL USEFULNESS.

" 1. It is a remedy against barrenness in woman and in beasts.

"2. It is a preservation from sickness.

"3. It heals the infirmities both of the mind and of the body.

"4. It purifies infected air and drives away plague and contagion."

Now can any one fail to see that this remarkable document, authorized by the Papal authorities of Rome, does most distinctly and explicitly attribute to their holy water, influences, etc. that belong to the Holy Spirit only? And is not the inference a legitimate one, that Romanism having lost the Spirit, has substituted water in its stead?

And now the question arises, From whence did this silly practice come? Surely not from the Bible. Not a single passage can be adduced from the word of God to support such a blasphemous ceremony. What then was its origin? The answer to this question is plain. It came from heathendom, the cesspool of religious abominations. It has no higher origin. It is a Pagan rite, that should have been left for only heathens to practise, instead of being incorporated among the rites of the Church to disgrace her service.

The Jesuit la Cerda, in his note on a passage in Virgil where this practice is mentioned as prevalent among Pagans, says: "Hence was derived the custom of the holy Church to provide purifying or holy water at the entrance of

Holy Water a Pagan Rite. 191

their churches."* Besides all this, it is a notorious fact that Roman Catholic priests and bishops prepare their holy water by putting in salt, and consecrating the mixture with religious ceremonies very much in the same manner that heathen priests mix and consecrate theirs.

Every one acquainted with the various systems of the idolatrous rites and ceremonies of Pagan nations, knows how generally *holy water* was used by them in their devotions. The *Sintoists* of Japan, who are regarded as the devotees of the most ancient system of idolatry among that people, have their *holy water* in the outer court of their temples, which is applied to their persons before proceeding further with their devotions, very much as Roman Catholic churches have their fonts of holy water at their entrances for the use of their communicants before entering. The similarity in this respect between one of these Pagan temples and a Roman Catholic church is very striking, and cannot fail to impress the mind with the heathen origin of the whole affair. The Hindoos also had their *holy water*, the Ganges, which they used for very much the same purpose that Papists use their holy water. The Hindoos claim that it heals the sick, and purifies the soul, besides doing many other wonderful things. Hence it is carried to immense distances to be

* Mystery of Iniquity Unvailed, p. 241.

kept as a dispeller of evil influences. Its waters are said to purify from every stain the person who undergoes a proper ablution. Hence journeys are taken of thousands of miles by such as have the means and the leisure, for the purpose of bathing in its waters. Temples are erected on its banks where hundreds of pilgrims from the surrounding country are daily performing their devotions by the use of this holy water. To die on its banks, wet by its waters, is believed to be a sure passport to Paradise. For this reason many devotees yield themselves to a voluntary death amid its waves. With such reverence is it regarded, that it is said that the Courts of Bengal use the waters of the Ganges to swear their witnesses over, just as our Courts use the Bible. It is also said that where the waters of this sacred river cannot be had, the Buddhist priests consecrate water by prayers and ceremonies, and sell it to the people as holy water to protect them from the evils of life, and that they often sprinkle it upon the sick and dying. Water thus consecrated is believed by these Pagans to possess supernatural properties; hence their great reverence for it. But what shall we say of Roman Catholics, who profess to be enlightened by the rays of divine truth, following so closely in the footsteps of ignorant and superstitious heathens, who are groping their way amid the

Holy Water a Pagan Rite. 193

darkness of idolatry? Romish priests, who ought to know better, and who ought to be heartily ashamed of this Pagan superstition, are found, by prayers and ceremonies, making *holy water*, for the ignorant, superstitious devotees of their faith, to carry to their homes, to be placed in their rooms, or under their pillows, and to sprinkle on their persons and about their dwellings for the purpose of protecting them from heathen influences, just as heathens do; but that they should sanction this Pagan rite by carrying it to the ridiculous extent of sprinkling the dead, is truly astonishing.

The heathens had their holy water because they had nothing better. They had by tradition received a knowledge of their defilement, and their consequent need of purification, and consequently, in their blindness, they applied to the creature instead of the Creator. As water was the great purifier for physical impurities, it was readily conceived that by the infusion of a supernatural quality through the ceremony, and prayer of consecration by a priest or some divinity, it then would cleanse the soul. This idea has been well nigh universal in heathen lands. We meet with it in ancient Egypt. They had their sacred Nile, which was regarded with the same superstitious reverence by them as the Ganges was by the Hindoos. This was what made the plague by which the waters of the Nile were turned to blood so great a calamity to Pharaoh and his people. The Thibetians, in their worship of the Grand Lama, have among their rites the use of *holy water* prepared and used very much as in Hindostan. Mahomet, who, in forming a new system of religion, drew largely on Paganism for materials, did not forget their holy water. Accordingly the waters of the well *Zem Zem* were consecrated to religious purposes, which it is affirmed are not only efficacious for curing many bodily diseases, but also for healing all spiritual disorders, and even procuring an absolute remission of sins. This water is conveyed by pilgrims in bottles to all parts of the Mahomedan dominions, to protect them against all manner of evil.

Now, can any one fail to see from whence Rome obtained her idea of *holy water*, and her teachings respecting its efficacy to heal diseases, expel devils, and cleanse the soul? It must certainly be admitted that she has not only borrowed this nonsensical practice from Paganism, but that she has, in this respect, followed remarkably close in its footsteps. She has, to a great extent, substituted *holy water* in the place of the Holy Ghost.

The Bible, which so expressly and pointedly condemns the whole system of image worship as held by Rome, and which must ever in its teachings oppose the use of *holy water*, or any other Pagan rite that would in any measure usurp the prerogatives of the Holy Ghost, can never be held by Romanists in the high estimation it deserves. Hence her opposition to the Bible.

CHAPTER XVIII.

Paganism of Popery.—Her Candle Burning.

ANOTHER Pagan characteristic of Rome, and perfectly in keeping with the foregoing, is her constant use of candles at masses, at the sacraments, at the benedictions, and at processions. They are seen everywhere on her altars in greater or less numbers, according to the *eclat* of the occasion. One of her feast days, called *Candlemass-day*, is held annually on the 2d of February, at which time all the wax candles and tapers which are used during the year are consecrated. At Rome the consecration of candles is performed by the Pope. Like holy water, they are supposed to be particularly offensive to evil spirits, and are used to keep them away. This fact is brought forth distinctly in the form or prayer of candle-consecration, which in part is as follows: "O Lord Jesus Christ, bless thou this creature of a *waxen taper* at our humble supplication, and by virtue of the holy cross pour thou into it an heavenly benediction; that thou hast granted it unto man's use for the expelling of darkness, it may receive such a strength and blessing, through the token of the holy cross, that in what places soever it be lighted or set, *the Devil may avoid out of these habitations, and tremble for fear, and fly away discouraged, and presume no more to unquiet them that serve thee,"* etc.*

It is wonderful that educated men, with the Bible in their hands, professing to be the ambassadors of Christ, should so far forget the dignity of their office and position, as to stoop to such nonsensical foolery. Where is there any authority for this in the inspired volume? Where is there the least intimation of the efficacy of candle-burning in any shape? Did Christ or his Apostles ever pray over, or consecrate candles? There is not a particle of evidence that they ever done any such thing. It would have been the merest trifling; and what is it but mockery for any one to pray to God to bless a candle, so as by virtue of the holy cross, to pour into it a heavenly benediction (whatever that may mean), so that the Devil may fear it, so as not only to tremble, but to be frightened away. By this arrangement, according to this theory, the Devil can be so effectually kept at a distance that the command of the Saviour to watch and pray that ye enter not into temptation, is made unnecessary, as the thing can be accomplished by this candle arrangement with much less trouble to the individual. But to be serious, what a fearful re-

* Mass-book, 1554.

sponsibility must rest upon those who are guilty of instituting such absurd rites for the observance of Christians in the place of the injunctions and teachings of the Scriptures!

No one acquainted with ancient heathen mythology can be at a loss for a moment as to the origin of this Candle-mass festival. In fact the burning of candles, lamps, or tapers, in Pagan temples, has been nearly universal.

This heathen practice is traced back to the early history of the Egyptians, who had their yearly festival of the *lighting of candles* somewhat similar to that of Rome.* Herodotus, who lived nearly five hundred years before Christ, tells us that the Egyptians (who first introduced the use of lights or lamps into their temples) had a famous yearly festival, called from the principal ceremony of it, *the lighting up of candles.*†

The ancient Greeks and Romans also had their sacred lights. In the festival of Pagan Rome, which was celebrated yearly in honor of the god Saturn, the temple of this deity which stood in the Roman forum, was gorgeously lighted up by a great number of "*wax tapers.*"‡

Among the Chinese, who are perhaps the most ancient nation upon the globe, and who are proverbial for their adherence to old cus-

---
* Enc. Amer., vol. xi., p. 211.
† Herodotus, book ii., vol. i, p. 277. London Edition.
‡ Enc. Amer., vol. xi., p. 211.

toms, there is celebrated yearly the feast of *Lanterns*. Besides, their Pagodas (temples), which are almost innumerable, and which contain their idols, are illuminated with a vast variety of *lamps which are kept burning without intermission day and night*.

In Tartary, where it is said their idolatrous system is of three thousand years standing, the Grand Lama, the object of their religious homage, is represented as sitting in his palace, cross-legged on a cushion, decked with gold and precious stones, "*amid a great number of burning lamps.*"

The truth is, if any one of the customs of idolatrous worship might be regarded as more purely Pagan, it would seem that the burning of lamps, candles, or tapers, as a religious ceremony, might well claim this distinction. Luctantius, who flourished in the beginning of the fourth century, is quoted by a certain author as saying: "Seemeth he to be in his right mind who offereth up to the Giver of all light a *wax candle* for a gift! . . . Their (the heathen) gods, because they be earthly, have need of light, lest they remain in darkness; whose worshipers, because they understand no heavenly thing, do draw religion, which they use, down to earth." Who also adds: "Thus far Luctantius, and much more of candle-lighting in temples before images and idols for religion;

whereby appeareth both the foolishness thereof, and also that in opinion and act we do agree altogether in our *candle religion with the Gentile idolaters.*"

Here is not only direct testimony that *candle worship* was idolatrous in its origin, but also that it was from heathendom, and had begun to make its appearance in the church even at that time. This evil continued to grow until in the year 641, when Pope Sergius declared the *burning of candles* to be an essential part of their worship, and appointed the Candle-mass festival. That this festival was borrowed from the heathens, as before stated, is evident from the fact that it corresponds with the *Februan* purification rights of Paganism, as described by Ovid. Besides the Pope appointed this festival on the very same day (2d February) that the Pagans held theirs. That this is the true origin of the whole of this superstitious system of candle-burning foolery, is evident from the following explanation given by Pope Innocent III. as an apology for the practice:

"Why do we carry lighted candles at this festival? The answer may be derived from the Book of Wisdom where it is said (ch. xiv., 23) that the *heathen offered sacrifices at night.* The Gentiles indeed had devoted the month of February to the infernal deities, because, as they ignorantly believed, it was at the beginning of this month that Pluto had ravished Proserpine. Ceres, her mother, had, according to their belief, sought her through Sicily for a whole night by the light of torches kindled at the flames of Etna. In commemoration of this, they every year, at the beginning of February, traveled the city during the night, bearing lighted torches, whence this festival was called *amburbale* (fire-procession). But the holy fathers *being unable to abolish this custom, decided that lighted candles should be carried in honor of the blessed, Virgin Mary ;* and thus what was formerly done for *Ceres* is done to-day in honor of the *Virgin,* and what was done formerly for *Proserpine* is now done in the praise of *Mary.**

Here we have the pitiful acknowledgment, and that from the Pope himself, the highest authority in the Roman Catholic Church, that the whole of this candle-blessing and candle-burning business, that forms such a conspicuous figure in the religious ceremonies of their church, has no higher origin than heathendom; and that it was originally founded in falsehood. Mark you, the Pope does not even claim that the practice is in any way as much as countenanced by the word of God. The truth is, the whole arrangement of candle-burning, as practised by the Romish Church, is a system of gross idolatry, borrowed directly, as we have seen, from Pagans, according to their own acknowledgment. That mankind should have originally, after losing a knowledge of the true God, been led to worship the sun, moon and

* Bib. Theol. Ec. Cyc., Vol. ii., p. 70.

stars, and finally to worship fire as emblems of these luminaries, is not so strange ; but that a church professing to be Christian should continue this ridiculous farce, that has no higher origin than the grossly absurd and licentious vagaries of heathen mythology, is a burning shame, and a living scandal to the Romish Church. No wonder a sect practising such heathenish customs and idolatrous rights should seek to withhold the Bible from the masses. The inevitable result of a general knowledge of the Scriptures would be to expose to the people the unscriptural and Pagan character of Popery.

CHAPTER XIX.

Paganism of Popery.—The Origin of Monkery.

ANOTHER evidence that the Romish Church has drawn largely upon Paganism for her peculiar and anti-scriptural rites, etc., is found in her ascetic practices and institutions, such as her monastic orders, her theory of penance, etc., as well as the celibacy of the clergy.

Monastic seclusion dates even back to the fabulous ages of antiquity, and gave rise to the most ancient Oriental philosophy.

In Hindoostan, where no one can question the great antiquity of their religious teachings and customs, these heathens carry this doctrine of asceticism to such an extent as not only to teach the virtue of seclusion from society as a means of propitiating their gods, Brahma, Vishnu, and Siva, but also in many instances to put themselves beyond the pale and reach of mankind by committing suicide, as a religious duty.

Long before the time of Buddha Sakia, or Holy Sakia, (who, according to Sir William Jones, and other Oriental scholars, who have examined the subject, was born about one thousand years before the Christian era), Asceticism was even then a common practice. Hindoo devotees frequently retired from all society, and buried themselves in the depths of forests, in caves, and the most secluded places to be found, where they devoted themselves to the mortification of the senses, to painful penances, and to the performances of their superstitious rites, as the proper course to be pursued in order to become one with the Supreme Mind. These persons frequently gained such a reputation for holiness, that hundreds flocked to hear them, so that in this way religious communities grew up in these former desolate regions. The greater their voluntary afflictions, the greater their reputed purity. This was the legitimate result of their theory, which was that each individual sin must be expiated by a corresponding amount of pain and prayer. Hence the more intense and protracted their self-inflicted tortures, the more complete the atonement. In view of this, many racked their brains to invent more painful sufferings than had been endured by their comrades, the details of which, in many instances, are too revolting and horrifying to be described.

The most ancient religious order among the Chinese, called *Tao-tse*, place the supreme duty and felicity of man in a perfect state of tranquillity and indifference to the world, and were strictly speaking seclusionists, or *monks*, who avoided every kind of society as injurious to their religious vows. The followers of *Fo*, who profess to have received their religious system from the ancient Hindoos, teach "that the sum of virtue and happiness is to be found in indolence and immobility, in the cessation of bodily motion, the suspension of all mental faculties, the obliteration of all feelings and desires." Who does not see in a devotee of Fo all the essential characteristics of a Roman monk?

Even the Essenes (Therapeutæ), who were more than eighteen hundred years ago scattered over Syria, Egypt, and the neighboring countries, and who were more Pagan than any thing else, were ascetics. They thought that religion consisted in silence and meditation. This people are supposed by Mosheim to "have borrowed their *monkish* notions from the Egyptians."

The Gnostic heresy that crept into the church in the first century was also the leaven of heathen asceticism, that had been drawn from the Grecian philosophy of Pythagoras and Plato.

In Japan, however, we have the system of heathen monkery in a regularly organized form. The Buddhists of that ancient people, a religious order, have, generally, close by, or in the neighborhood of their pagods, their convents filled with monks. In fact, among these heathens, there are various orders of Pagan hermits. One of these is the *Bikunis* order, which consists of mendicant *nuns*, very much resembling the ancient nuns of Venus.*

In the Pagan institutions of Thibet, as published in Green's Collection of Voyages, where they boast of their religious system as being three thousand years old, "they have a vast number of convents, filled with *monks* and friars, amounting to thirty thousand." It is said that the city of Lassa alone contains no less than three thousand monastic establishments, called Lamaseries (from Lama Shepherd). These institutions, that so strikingly resemble the monasteries and nunneries that are found in all Roman Catholic countries, are usually built on hills or mountains, in most commanding situations, and are generally large and imposing structures. Some of them are occupied by sisterhoods of women who have devoted themselves to ascetic rites, to attain a higher state of holiness. All who accept this mode of life adopt a vow of celibacy, separate themselves from the world, shave their heads, and change their names. Here mortification of the senses and penance are duly practiced; beads are counted in connection with their supplications, and prayers offered for the repose of departed souls. Here images, amulets, and holy water,

* See C. A. Goodrich's Rel. Cer., p. 531.

The Origin of Monkery. 207

are consecrated and distributed to the faithful, as essential helps to a holy life. In fact, so remarkable is the similarity between these heathen institutions and Roman Catholic monasteries, that when Father Huc, a French Jesuit, visited that country some years ago, in his report of what he saw, etc., he says:

"The reception given us recalled to our thoughts those monasteries raised by our own religious ancestors, in which travelers and the poor always found refreshment for the body, and consolation for the soul."

He also tells us that when he tried to persuade the Regent of Lassa, to become a Roman Catholic, he listened courteously, and then replied: "*Your religion is the same as ours.*"

When Borri, a Jesuit missionary, visited these countries, he was forcibly struck with the same resemblance, and says:

"It looks as if the Devil had endeavored to represent among the Gentiles the beauty and variety of *religious orders* in the Catholic Church. * * * If any man came newly into that country, he might easily be persuaded there had been Christians there in former times, *so nearly has the Devil attempted to imitate us.*"

If he had said so nearly have we imitated the Devil, he would have been much nearer the truth.

When Mexico was first visited by the Spaniards under Cortez, in 1521, and its capital captured after a siege of seventy-five days, with a most dreadful slaughter, it was found that such was the devotion of these heathens to their superstitious rites and customs, that in the city of Mexico itself there were more than a thousand temples, and some five thousand priests, and adds the historian, " They likewise had *monastic orders*, especially one into which no person was admitted under sixty years of age."*

From all this, it is not difficult to understand the origin of monkery. Hence, during the first three hundred years of Christianity it was unknown. Anthony the Hermit, who died in 356, was the first. His example was soon followed by others. As the period of darkness, superstition, and idolatry which followed, had commenced to cast its shadows, heathen customs and institutions began to revive. The doctrine of justification by faith was laid aside for the old heathen asceticism, or doctrine of merit by suffering. In consequence of this, monkery increased with an astonishing rapidity. Monks soon came up upon the whole land like the frogs of Egypt. The Popes seeing that it could be turned to good account in increasing their power, took it under their fostering care. But where is there any authority for this in the teachings of Christ or his Apostles?

The same may be said of the whole system of

* Goodrich's Rel. Cer. p. 564.

penance, as taught and practiced by the Romish Church. Every one acquainted with the religious systems of heathens knows how universal was this practice. This heathen custom has been one of the leading features of paganism, and consequently has been handed down to the present time, so that all the countries which profess the religion of Brahma, Fo, Lama, and Mohammed, are full of fakirs and santons, tanirs, or songesses, talapoins, bonzes, and dervises, who are devotees of fanatical and absurd penances.*

Notwithstanding its pagan character and origin, such was the ignorance and corruption of the Romish Church, that penance was not only adopted so as to absolutely supersede the necessity of faith as necessary to justification and adoption, but this gross absurdity has by Rome been exalted to the sanctity of a sacrament. And such have been the virtues ascribed to penance by the hierarchy of that church, that its votaries soon vied with the Hindoo, worshipers of Siva in the horrid tortures to which they subjected themselves as meritorious acts. In the eleventh century, voluntary flagellations were superadded to increase the sum of their sufferings. In Italy, "Nobles and peasants, old and young, even children of five years of age, whose only covering was a cloth tied round the

* See Encyc. Amer., Vol. VIII., p. 571.

middle, went in pairs, by hundreds, thousands, and tens of thousands, through the towns and villages, visiting the churches in the depth of winter. Armed with scourges, they flogged each other without pity, and the streets resounded with *cries and groans that drew tears from all who heard them.*"*

Surely there is nothing like this in the teachings of Christ and his Apostles. Jesus says: "My yoke is *easy* and my burden is *light.*" The Saviour rebuked the Pharisees for binding *heavy burdens upon men*, but as wicked as they were, they never began to equal the Romanists in this respect. As we have seen, the practice is of heathen origin. It belongs to a state of darkness, ignorance and superstition. The attempt of Romanists to support this pagan custom by translating Μετανοια (*repentance*), *doing penance*, will not answer. To say nothing of the fact that the classical usage of the word is altogether against such a rendering, *doing penance* not being even one of its meanings,† it makes nonsense of most of the passages in which the word occurs, such as, "There is joy in heaven over one sinner that *does penance.* God commands all men to *do penance.* Except ye *do penance*, ye shall all likewise perish. He is not willing that any should perish, but that all should

---
* D'Aubigne His. of Ref., Vol. I., p. 54.
† See Donnegan's, Grove's and Pickering's Greek and English Lexicons.

return *to penance,*" etc., etc. What a translation! How ridiculously absurd! And yet the Douay Bible has this translation of the word Μετανοια wherever it occurs in the New Testament, except one. Now who does not see that a man may *do penance*, and yet neither repent nor reform? Besides, this unwarrantable rendering makes the devotees of Brahma, who are as severe in their practices of *doing penance* as are Romanists, as acceptable to God as the best Papists. Can any thing be more absurd than this heathenish dogma of Rome?

CHAPTER XX.

The Paganism of Popery.—Purgatory and Canonized Saints.

ANOTHER of the many errors of the Roman Catholic Church is her anti-scriptural doctrine of purgatory. This is a third place, as they hold, in which departed souls are confined, who are not deserving of eternal damnation, nor yet fit for heaven. In this middle place it is affirmed they are confined until they are purified by its fires and the prayers of friends, for the abodes on high.

But from whence is this doctrine obtained? The Bible speaks only of two places beyond the grave—*heaven* and *hell*. It says not one word about a third, where souls are purified by fire and the prayer of saints. There is not a single intimation throughout the inspired record, that the condition of any departed soul can possibly be affected by any amount of suffering, or any thing that we can do. Besides, this Romish dogma is in direct opposition to the teachings of the Bible. It teaches that the purgation of sin is *after death;* the Bible teaches that, if done at all, it is done in *this life*. The doctrine of purgatory teaches that this cleansing is done by *fire ;* the Bible tells us that *the blood of Jesus Christ* cleanses from sin. Rome tells us that the fires of purgatory will ultimately be extinguished; the Bible assures us that the fires of punishment are everlasting. Romanists believe that the fires of purgatory are prepared for the purification of saints who, because of unavoidable imperfections, are unfit to enter heaven; while the Bible teaches us that all the fire in the other world was prepared for the devil and his angels; besides John says: "The blood of Jesus Christ, his Son, cleanseth us from all sin." Hence, nothing left for fire to do. If Christ died for us and redeemed us from sin and hell, as the Scriptures assure us, then the idea of further meritorious sufferings detracts from the perfection of Christ's work, and places merit still in the creature, in direct opposition to the positive declaration of God's word.

When our Saviour was expiring on the cross, he exclaimed, "it is finished;" but if the doctrine of purgatory is true, the expiation of sin was only then begun, and which was to be completed in purgatory. Jesus Christ says one thing, and Romanists say another. The Bible teaches us that if men die in their sins they must perish, but Popery inculcates the belief of a *post mortem* repentance and purification of sin. The Bible informs us that the saints are to sing "unto him that loved us, and washed us from our sins in his own blood," etc., whereas if this doctrine be true, the ascription of the saints will be unto purgatory that has purified us, be glory, etc.

Is it any wonder that Romanists seek to keep the Bible from the eyes of the people? Who does not see that a knowledge of the Bible would at once reveal the anti-scriptural character of Popery?—that purgatory, so far from being a Bible doctrine, is directly in conflict with the Bible?

Purgatory is of heathen origin. The doctrine of a future state of purification was connected by the ancient Egyptians with their theory of the transmigration of souls. We also find it in the heathen mythology of the ancient Grecians. They believed that Charon, one of their deities, who was represented under the form of an old man with white hair, and long flowing beard, was the ferryman to ferry ghosts over the four rivers of hell, preparatory to their entering the palace of Pluto; and, that none could pass over immediately, or even enter Charon's boat without his permission, which depended upon certain qualifications. In case they were unfit to pass over, they were left to wander amid the mud and slime of the shore for a hundred years.*

Homer also, in his twelfth book of the Odys-

* See Virgil's Eneid, Book vi.

sey, recognizes a middle state, or purgatory, and that the souls therein detained were benefitted by the prayers, alms and sacrifices of their pious friends.

" Eusebius relates of Plato (a heathen) that he divided mankind into three states; some, who, having purified themselves by philosophy, and excelled in holiness of life, enjoy an eternal felicity in the islands of the blessed without any labor or trouble, which neither is it possible for any words to express, nor any thoughts to conceive. Others, that had lived exceedingly wicked, and who therefore seemed incapable of cure, he supposed were at their death thrown down headlong into hell, there to be tormented forever. But now, besides these, he imagined there was a middle sort, who, though they had sinned, yet had repented of it, and therefore seemed to be in a curable condition ; and these, he thought, went down for some time, to hell too, to be purged and absolved by grievous torments; but that after that they should be delivered from it, and attain to honor according to the dignity of their benefactors."*

From the above it is plainly seen where the idea of purgatory was obtained by the Papists. Indeed Cardinal Ballarmine, when called upon by circumstances to furnish authority for the Romish belief in purgatory, actually founded his argument on this very fact, that the heathens believed it.

This doctrine of a middle state has been very general among pagans, both in ancient and

* McGavin's Prot. vol. 1, page 54.

modern times, especially among the Hindoos, Japanese, and Thibetians.

In Hindostan, Buddha Sakia, which means the Holy Sakia, or Saint Sakia, inculcated this doctrine of a sort of purgatory near three thousand years ago. He was believed to be an incarnation of Vishnu, the second person in the Hindostan trinity, and that he came into this world to subject himself to severe penances that he might expiate the sins of mankind by suffering; and that he descended into hell to deliver them who were expiating their offences by the pains of purgatory. His followers also taught that if a man afflicted himself more than was necessary, or repeated more prayers than were required to expiate his own offences, or more of both, that the overplus could be used for deceased relatives or friends, by being placed to their account, so as to diminish their torments, or if the amount was sufficient, to end them. Hence many rich men sought to obtain the rewards of Paradise by leaving large bequests for the erection of temples or other religious institutions, where prayers might be said for their souls after death, that their sufferings by these means might be greatly shortened.

The doctrine of a future purification, says a German Catholic writer,* "was closely connected by the ancients with that of the transmigra-

* Encyc. Amer. vol. x, p. 429.

tion of souls, which, as it first prevailed among the Egyptians, was not hingmore than a symbolical representation of the immortality of the soul. Succeeding philosophers made use of this doctrine of transmigration, to deter rude tribes from sin, by connecting their future condition with that of various species of animals, which was well fitted to strike unreflecting natures. It was afterwards *unhappily chosen* to indicate the mode of the purification of the soul, and its preparation for the joys of heaven."

The Pope seeing how greatly this doctrine might be made to contribute to the power of the Papacy, should it be adopted with the necessary improvements to make it efficient as an auxiliary to his greatness, at once declared it to be a dogma of the church. It was immediately invested with every circumstance calculated to impress the minds of the ignorant and superstitious with its wonderful character. The Popes claimed to preside over purgatory with plenary power. It was declared that an immense treasure of merit, consisting in part of the blood of Christ, that had been, as was declared, shed unnecessarily, and also the unnecessary works of saints, which they did over and beyond what was their duty, called works of supererogation, had been committed to them to be applied to such as were confined in purgatory, and, where, without these merits, they must suffer immensely for a long period before they would be sufficiently purified by mere fire to enter heaven. The people were taught that for a certain sum of money they could have their departed friends delivered from these torments. In order to increase the revenues of the hierarchy, pictures were suspended in their churches, representing the souls of individuals weltering in fire, that could at once be released by the requisite amount of gold.

About in keeping with the above anti-scriptural and absurd dogma, is the Popish practice of supplication to departed saints. As to the origin of this abomination there can be no doubt. Every student knows that the gods of Greece and Rome were deified heroes—canonized according to the customs of the times. This prominent feature of pagan superstition has been with some slight changes incorporated into the system of Popery. As the heathens had gods to guard their every interest, so the Romish Church decided to have her tutelary divinities, too, in the form of canonized saints. At the head of the Papal mythology was placed the Virgin Mary, who became to them very much what Diana was to the Ephesians. Her image was set up in every temple. In honor of her were instituted the rosary and the crown. She was more honored than Christ. The list of glorified saints became preposterously multiplied. Each canonization, however, brought large sums into the treasury, and the system was encouraged. The canonizing of P. de Alcantara and Maria M. de Pazzi by Clement IX., amounted to no less than sixty-four thousand dollars. Many of those raised to this dignity were of very questionable character. In the thirteenth century a dualist came very near being canonized. In the same century A. Pungilovo died, over whose tomb an altar was built, and in whose honor statues were erected in the churches throughout the diocese in which he lived. Even miracles, it was affirmed, were wrought at his tomb. The bishop and chapter investigated the miracles and declared them to be "*genuine.*" It was determined to canonize him, but in the investigation of his life they found him to be so unfit for this promotion that instead of canonizing him, they dug up his bones and burnt them.* How humiliated must have been the churches that had his statues, and the bishop that affirmed that miracles were wrought at his tomb! Who does not see the gross imposition as well as the foolery of this whole system? And yet the Council of Trent enjoined the "*worship of canonized saints* by all her communicants." What is this but downright idolatry? What better is it than the worshiping of deified heroes, such as was

* See B. T. Ec. Cyc., v. ii., p. 91.

practiced by the ancient heathens? Is it any wonder that a church that enjoins such anti-scriptural and absurd practices upon her members, should seek to keep the Bible out of their hands, and out of the hearing of their children in the public schools ? Christ has truly said : *"Every one that doeth evil hateth the light, neither cometh to the light lest his deeds should be reproved."*

The pagan character of Rome, which is unquestionably the secret of her persistent hostility to the circulation of the Scriptures among the people, is seen not only in her worship of pictures and images—her constant use of holy water—her burning candles upon her altars—her monastic orders—her system of penance—her doctrine of celibacy—her teachings of purgatory—her supplication to saints, but also in her many other peculiar customs and ceremonies, which find no warrant in, or authority from the word of God, such as her doctrine of auricular confessions—her numerous feasts—her canonization of saints—her fasts and use of beads—her devotion to relics—her earthly head—her mitred prelates—her robed priests—her crosiers—her palliums—her scrap-altars, etc. Where is the authority of all these save in the heathen rites and ceremonies of a blind and corrupt superstition ?

Just in proportion as the Romish Church lost

the inner life of Christianity, she sought to increase her power by extending her conquests over the surrounding pagan nations. To accomplish this, she sought to make the transition from paganism to Christianity easy by adopting pagan rites, symbols, festivals, and ceremonies, until paganism has become her leading feature.

CHAPTER XXI.

Roman Despotism.

EVERY one familiarly acquainted with the past history of the Roman Catholic Church, and unbiassed by prejudice or interest, must have been deeply impressed with the absolute despotism that has been inaugurated and maintained with all the attendants of the most unscrupulous policy of a worldly ambition, by her, during the whole period of her greatest prosperity. Popes and Councils have seemed to vie with each other in seeking to crush out every appearance of liberal principles, or independence among the nations of the earth, to the extent of their power. In violation of the plainest teachings of Christ, they have claimed authority from heaven to overturn every kingdom that should dare to oppose their extravagant assumptions, and to bring all men into subordination to their iron yoke.

Pope Boniface VIII., in a bull called *Unam Sanctum*, utters the following language: "We declare and determine it a principle absolutely necessary to salvation that all human beings are subject to the Pope." And mind you, this subjection is not merely ecclesiastical subjection, but is intended to include political subjection also, entire and complete. The same Pope in a letter addressed to Philip, King of France, declares "that all kings and persons whatever, and the King of France as well as others, by divine command owe perfect obedience to the Roman pontiff; and this not merely in religious matters, but likewise in secular and human affairs." In the *Dictates* drawn up by Pope Gregory VII., it is declared among other things that "it is lawful for the Pope to depose emperors, and absolve subjects from their allegiance to unrighteous rulers." Pope Martin V., in sending ambassadors to Constantinople, headed their instructions as follows: "THE MOST HOLY AND MOST BLESSED, WHO IS LORD ON EARTH, THE MASTER OF THE UNIVERSAL WORLD, THE MOST HIGH AND SOVEREIGN BISHOP, MARTIN, BY DIVINE PROVIDENCE," &c.

Such is in perfect harmony with the blasphemous salutations of Romanists, "*Noster Dominus Deus papa.*" *The Lord our God the Pope*, as they bow down and kiss his feet. What is this but accepting divine honor?

These absurd pretensions and ungodly assumptions, have been rigidly carried out to the utmost extent of their power, by thundering the dire and tremendous anathemas on the heads of all who ventured to think for themselves, or question their right to rule the world. While they profess to be the Vicegerents of Christ, who declared his kingdom not of this world, they have sought not only to lord it over God's heritage, but to rule with a rod of iron over all the kingdoms of the earth.

The haughty pretensions of Pope Innocent III., are unsurpassed for pride, arrogance and lordly utterances. In his coronation sermon he said: "Now you may see who is the servant who is placed over the family of the Lord; truly is he the Vicar of Jesus Christ, the successor of Peter, the Christ of the Lord, the God of Pharaoh; placed in the middle between God and man, on this side of God, but beyond man; less than God but greater than man; who judges all, but is judged of none." Here we have the incarnation of the most despotic assumtions that it is possible for a man to avow. Nor was this mere empty declamation. He created kings both in Europe and Asia according to his pleasure. In Asia he gave a king to the Armenians. In Europe he conferred the honors of royalty on Primislaus, the Duke of Bohemia; and also by his legate he placed a royal crown on Johannicius, duke of the Bulgarians; and in person, crowned at Rome, Peter II. of Aragon.

It is almost incredible to read the terror and consternation that were excited among all ranks in the middle ages by Papal maledictions and excommunications.

Among those who fell under the displeasure of the Popes may be named the Emperor Henry IV., and also Henry VI., Emperor; Leopold, Duke of Austria; Alphonson X., King of Galicia; Philip Augustus, King of France; Frederick II., Emperor of Germany; Philip the Fair, King of France; Lewis XII., also King of France; John and Henry VIII., both Kings of England; also Queen Elizabeth; Joan, Queen of Navarre; and Basilius, King of Poland.

Henry IV., Emperor of Germany, was formally deposed by Pope Gregory VII., and his subjects absolved from their oath of allegiance to him as their sovereign in the following language:

"For the dignity and defense of God's holy Church, in the name of the Father, Son and Holy Ghost, I depose from imperial and royal administration, King Henry, son of Henry, some time Emperor, who too boldly and rashly laid hands on the Church. I absolve all Christians subject to the Empire from that oath, whereby they were wont to plight their faith unto true kings; for it is right that he should be deprived of dignity who doth endeavor to diminish the majesty of the Church."

As this did not bring the king to terms, the Pope three years after pronounced another terrible curse upon him.

The same calamity was visited upon Frederick II., another German Emperor, by Pope Innocent IV. When Basilius, King of Poland, was hurled from his throne by Pope Gregory VII., he not only dissolved the oath of allegiance of his subjects, but by imperious edict, prohibited the nobles and clergy from electing a new king without his consent. Pope Paul III. deposed Henry VIII., King of England, after this style: "I absolve all his subjects from their oath of allegiance to him, and command them all, under pain of excommunication, not to obey him, nor any officer under him."

In about the same style was Queen Elizabeth of England cursed, and excommunicated by Pius V., because she dared to be a Protestant. The anathema, which was pronounced in the following language, shows at once the unbounded despotism and wrath that governed him :

"We (the Pope,) declare her to be deprived of her pretended title to the kingdom aforesaid, and all dominion, dignity and privilege whatsoever, and also the nobility, subjects and people of said kingdom, and all others which have in any sort sworn unto her; to be forever absolved from any such manner of duty, dominion, allegiance, and obedience; as we also do by these presents absolve them, and deprive Elizabeth of her pretended title to the kingdom, and all other things above said. And we command and interdict all and every, the noblemen, subjects and people, and others aforesaid, that they presume not to obey her, or her monitions, mandates or laws. And those that shall do contrary we include in the same sentence of condemnation."

And be it remembered that these anathemas were not merely harmless invectives to be despised and scorned as the ravings of pride, arrogance, and imbecility. Romanists believe that the Popes act by divine authority, and that they must be obeyed. When John, King of England, had offended Pope Innocent III., he laid his kingdom under an interdict, by which all the places of worship were shut up for "three years," and the "dead buried in the highways without the ordinary rights of interment." This failing to bring the King to terms, the Pope proceeded to severer measures. He absolved his subjects from their oath of allegiance, and declared his throne vacant, and called upon the King of France to enter upon the conquest of Briton, and to annex it to his own dominions. An army was immediately raised for this purpose, which, in connection with the wide-spread disaffection among his own subjects, so alarmed the King of England, that he hastened to do homage to the Pope, who, after five days, restored his crown and scepter upon the most humiliating conditions.

In fact, the most powerful monarchs were powerless before the Popes. Emperors led his horse and held his stirrup. Kings who chanced to fall under his displeasure, were stripped by him of their honors and power, and whole realms were deprived of every religious privilege. The Emperor Henry was not only driven from his throne by Pope Gregory VII., but compelled to cross the Alps amid the rigors of winter to implore the clemency of the Pope. On arriving at Canusium, the Pope's residence at that time, he was compelled to stand at the entrance of this fortress for three days, in the open air, with his feet bare, his head uncovered, and no other garment but a coarse woollen cloth thrown around his naked body.

For sanctioning, as was supposed, the assassination of Thomas A. Becket, Henry II., king of England, was compelled by Pope Alexander to walk barefoot over three miles of flinty road, with only a coarse cloth over his shoulders, to the shrine of Becket, where eighty monks, four bishops, abbots and other clergy, who were present, whipped his bare back with a knotted cord, compelled him to drink water mingled with blood, and to pay forty pounds a year for tapers to burn perpetually before the martyr's tomb.

Said Pope Boniface to Philip King of France: "We desire that thou shouldest know that thou art subject to us in ecclesiastical and worldly matters." "God has set us over kings and countries to tear down and destroy, spoil and scatter, build up and plant."

In fact, to such an extent of insanity was this idea of Papal authority over all mankind carried, that a provision was inserted in the canon law declaring that "if a Pope was so lost to the duties of his high station that through negligence he drew multitudes with him to hell, yet was he not to be reproved by any man; for he was to judge mankind, and not to be judged by man; therefore the nations were to pray for him, for on him their salvation depended next to God." An ecclesiastical Papal writer says: "The Pope is bound by no form of law; his pleasure is law." "The Pope makes right of that which is wrong, and can change the nature of things." "The Pope is all and over all; he can change square things into round." Pope Adrian VI. said to the Elector Frederick, whom he sought to intimidate, in order to prevent his encouraging or supporting the Reformation : "Thou art a sheep; presume not to impugn thy shepherd, nor to judge thy God and Christ." Could any form of words be employed more shocking or blasphemous than the above? The very throne and high prerogatives of the Almighty are assumed as belonging to a poor, weak, sinful man. But such is their boasted claim, and such has been their tyranny founded upon these wicked pretensions over the nations of the earth.

The whole history of the Church shows Romanism to be the very worst form of despotism under the sun. Nothing can exceed its haughty pretensions, or the arrogance and pride with which it has sought to subjugate the world to its iron sway. Consequently she has ever been the enemy of all liberal governments and free institutions. True to her nature and instincts, in all struggles for liberty, she always arrays herself on the side of oppression. She must, from her very structure and nature, be an enemy to our free institutions, and woe to our country and our liberties when Romanism becomes dominant in these United States.

CHAPTER XXII.

Rome Still Despotic.

WHEN we refer to the past history of the Romish Church to show the terrible, crushing despotism with which she has oppressed mankind in past ages, we are frequently met with the reply, True, but Rome has changed ; that she is no longer the tyrant she was in the days of Hildebrand ; that with the progress of civilization she has advanced in the direction of a more humane and liberal policy ; that, in fact, it was nearly impossible for her, amid the general diffusion of knowledge, to still adhere to the despotic dogmas of the dark ages.

Such persons should remember that Rome boasts of her immutability. That, however greatly society may change in customs and forms, she changes not. And, it must be admitted that in this respect she has wonderfully held her own.

Rome is as despotic to-day in heart and soul as she has been at any former period of her existence. This charge is not based upon the assertions of her enemies, but upon the declarations of her own expounders of her principles, and what is better, her long and uniform practice. Austria, France, Spain, Germany and Italy, all testify to her unwearied efforts to crush out the recent uprisings of their people for greater political liberty. Wherever the struggle has been inaugurated between despotism on the one hand, and freedom on the other, she has invariably taken her stand with the former. She is to-day waging a most vigorous war, in all her strongholds, against the advances of civilization.

In an article in the *Catholic World* on "Religious Liberty," for April last, the idea of improvement on the part of the Romish Church toward a more liberal and democratic policy in this or any other country, is not only absolutely denied, but it is also asserted that her despotism and intolerance must from her very nature remain the same in all ages, and consequently it is utterly useless to look or hope for a change. He says:

"To seek to modify the position and action of the Church, so as to force her to accept and conform to the dominant or popular tendency or passion of the age or nation, is to mistake her essential character and office, and to forget that her precise mission is to *govern all men and nations, kings and peoples, sovereigns and subjects*, and to conform them to the invariable and inflexible law of God, which she is appointed by God himself to declare and apply, and therefore to resist with all her might every passion or tendency of every age, nation, community, or individual, whenever and wherever it deviates from that law of which she is the guardian and judge. The church is instituted, as every Catholic who understands his religion believes, to guard and defend the rights of God on earth against any and every enemy, at all times, and in all places. She therefore does not and cannot accept, *or in any degree favor, liberty in the Protestant sense of liberty*, and if liberty in that sense be the true sense, the Protestant pretension cannot be successfully denied." * * * * *

" The Protestant experiment has demonstrated beyond question that the very things in the Catholic Church which are most offensive to this age, and for which it wages unrelenting war against her, are precisely those things it most needs for its own protection and safety. It needs, first of all, the Catholic Church, nay, the Papacy itself *to declare and apply the law of God to states and empires*, to sovereigns and subjects, kings and peoples, that politics may no longer be divorced from religion, but be rendered subsidiary to the spiritual, the eternal end of man, for which both individuals and society exist and civil governments are instituted. It needs the church to *declare and enforce the law, by such means as she judges proper*. . . . The present delusions of the loud-spoken nineteenth century *must give way before her*, as she once more stands forth in her true light, and her present enemies *must be vanquished*."

Here it is declared by one of their leading papers that the Roman Catholic hierarchy still believes it to be the mission of the Church " to govern all men and nations," as in former times, when kings and emperors who chanced to fall under the Pope's displeasure, were by him stripped of their power, and whole realms were deprived of every religious privilege. It is also here declared that Popery " cannot accept, or in any degree favor liberty in the Protestant sense of liberty ;" that is, our free institutions, both civil and ecclesiastical. This we firmly believed, but were scarcely prepared for such an open avowal of the fact by Romanists themselves. What think Protestants, who have fancied that Rome had changed from what she formerly was, of these plain and emphatic declarations, that " the present delusions (religious toleration) of the loud-boasting nineteenth century must give way before her," and " her present enemies (Protestants) must be vanquished?" How they are to be vanquished her past history tells. Such is the spirit of Rome to-day, as proclaimed by herself, and what would be her practice if she but had the power, it is not difficult to divine.

When Joseph II., Emperor of Austria, adopted, some three years ago, a more liberal system in the government of the empire, by which men might be allowed to speak and publish their own thoughts, and by which Protestants might be permitted to have their own schools, instead of being compelled to send their children to Catholic schools ; and which provided also that heretics (Protestants) should not be refused burial in Catholic cemeteries, when those heretics have no burial-ground of their own, etc., the Pope was filled with holy indignation. This

Rome Still Despotic. 235

just and righteous legislation, which filled the down-trodden masses with untold joy, and led to the illumination of the city of Vienna, and which was hailed throughout Christendom by all lovers of right and equity as an evidence of the final triumph of more liberal principles and policies, was denounced by the Roman hierarchy as a *horrible crime*. During the enactment of the several liberal measures, the church party, encouraged by the Pope, steadfastly resisted every change. The bishops and clergy boldly threatened the liberal party with all sorts of ecclesiastical penalties and disabilities for resisting the authority and policy of Rome.

This threat was accordingly fulfilled in the Bull or allocution of the Pope which speedily followed, in which he says : " You see, consequently, venerable brethren, how necessary it is strongly to reprove and *condemn those abominable laws* sanctioned by the Austrian Government, laws which are in flagrant contradiction with the doctrines of the Catholic religion."

Here we have in the ravings of the present Pope against the adoption of a more liberal system by the Austrian Emperor, the same despotic spirit that was exhibited in the eleventh century by Hildebrand. After enumerating the various reforms that tended to lighten the burdens of the people, he further says :

"We reprove and we condemn, by our Apostolic authority, the laws which we have enumerated, and everything general or special in those same laws or in matters which refer to ecclesiastical right which has been decreed, or attempted unjustly in any manner whatsoever, by the Austrian Government, or its subordinates, whomsoever they may be. In virtue of the same authority which appertains to us, we declare those decrees null and powerless in themselves, and in their effect, both as regards the present and the future."

In the history of Mexico we have another instance of the modern despotic spirit and practice of Popery. For three hundred years after the overthrow of the empire of Montezuma, in 1520, Rome, through Spanish Roman Catholic officials and her bishops and clergy, ruled the people as with a rod of iron. Their education was neglected—superstition was inculcated—they were ruthlessly despoiled of their rights, without redress; impoverished by an ecclesiastical system of extortion, to swell the immense revenues of the church; demoralized by an irreligious priesthood, and coerced by them into the most abject obedience through the Inquisition.

It is not, therefore, surprising that under this cruel despotism, the population, instead of steadily increasing, was found at the close of the Spanish rule to have diminished.

At length, however, the people began to awaken from their slumber. In 1810, the cry of liberty was raised, and for the next eleven years a fierce struggle was maintained against despotism, in which many brave hearts met a martyr's doom. These beginnings prepared the way for the political changes that have followed.

In 1821, they resolutely threw off the yoke of Spain. This resulted in a popular reaction against despotism. About this time, Bibles began to find their way among the people. The proximity of the United States also aided the cause of freedom.

A Republican party was accordingly organized for the avowed purpose of establishing and maintaining constitutional liberty on the basis of equal rights, and freedom to worship God according to the dictates of conscience. To accomplish this, however, much remained to be done. Although they had succeeded in throwing off the Spanish yoke, the galling chains of Popery still remained. The Romish hierarchy openly avowed itself a political party, and at once sought alliance with all the aristocratic elements in the land for the purpose of successfully resisting every measure of reform that tended to elevate the down trodden masses. The struggle now commenced in earnest between the Reform party on the one hand, and the Roman Catholic party on the other. The leading questions at issue, and which for a season trembled in the balance, were of the most momentous character. A Monarchy or a Republic? A hereditary, tyrannical, irresponsible aristocracy, or rulers selected from, and elected by the people? A spiritual despotism by a union of Church and State, or, a divorcement, separation and independence of civil and ecclesiastical institutions, together with freedom and religious toleration?

The final contest of this great struggle culminated in 1857, when the Romish church party was defeated. A constitution, modeled after our own, was adopted. In their declaration of principles they proclaimed as fundamental, that all men were born free; that the rights of man are the bases and objects of government; that free speech, a free press, free labor and the right of petition should be maintained, etc. The Romish priesthood, maddened to desperation, resorted to every expedient in their power to overturn this liberal system and to establish a despotic government. They excommunicated such as supported or accepted the constitution. This failing to produce a reaction, they inaugurated a civil war and furnished means to military leaders to conduct the campaign. But, in 1860, the church party was vanquished. The archbishop, bishops, their military chieftains and political leaders were banished as enemies to liberty. But their efforts were not ended. They sought assistance in Europe, and soon returned with a foreign prince and a French army to crush the spirit and institutions of liberty in their own country, to banish the Bible, and freedom to worship God according to the dictates of conscience, and to re-establish their former inquisitorial religious intolerance and despotism. But this scheme also failed. The French Emperor was compelled to withdraw his forces and Maximillian was slain. So the Republic of Mexico yet stands in spite of the Roman Catholic party. They did all that they could do under the circumstances, and failed to crush out liberty only because they lacked the power.

The Emperor of France, who was both a usurper and a despot, who betrayed in the most shameful manner the liberties of the nation, had all through the period of his reign the political and moral support of the Bishops and clergy of the Romish Church. To them he owes a debt of gratitude, which he has in some measure paid, in the help he has furnished the Pope of Rome, by furnishing French soldiers to support his authority.

The Republicans of Spain to-day find the most determined opposition to a liberal government from the same source.

The Bishops and clergy unanimously applauded the action of the Spanish government when it overthrew the constitution of the country, arrested and exiled most of the members of the Cortes, and returned to the most despotic principles of administration. The priest party, not satisfied with this, have been urging the Government to abolish altogether the representation of the people until they have finally succeeded in placing a King upon the throne.

In Italy the advances that have been made by the people toward more liberal principles, under the teachings of such men as Garibaldi, have been steadily resisted and denounced by the Pope and his Bishops, with threats and excommunications. Nothing is more evident than that the Romish hierarchy has not only no sympathy with the progress of freedom, but cherishes the most deadly hate toward any effort made in any nation to secure a more liberal policy. This is not only true in Europe, but also in the New World. In Brazil, Peru, Chili, and all the South American Republics, Rome has invariably been arrayed on the side of oppression.

In our great rebellion, that sought to prostrate our liberties in the very dust, by establishing one of the worst forms of despotism known on earth, in which " slavery, the sum of all villainies," was made the corner-stone ; and when the South was waging a most fearful war against the government of the United States for the accomplishment of its horrible purpose, and while all Europe stood breathless, waiting the result of the terrible conflict, the Pope of Rome, true to his instincts, and true to the despotism over which he presides, with undue haste, was first and foremost in formally expressing his sympathy for Jefferson Davis and his cause, and in acknowledging the independence of the South.

Perfectly in keeping with the above was the terrible demonstration of the Irish Catholics, in the New York riot against the enforcement of the draft to put down the rebellion. When those infuriated Papists swept like a whirlwind of desolation through the streets, marking their way with fire and slaughter, Archbishop Hughes not only recognized them as communicants of Rome, but addressed them as "his children." They and the Pope were working in harmony for the same end, viz.: the triumph of the Southern rebellion and the consequent overthrow of our free institutions.

In Rome, the seat of the Papacy, the paradise of Romanism—where Popery has done according to her own will without let or hindrance, what a sad spectacle has been presented to the eye! The reins of despotism were held by an all-powerful hand. Spies by day and by night surrounded the suspected. No citizen could leave the Pope's temporal dominion without permission, based upon a certificate from the priest that he was a good Papist. A word spoken in favor of liberty would be cause for arrest. In fact, as one of our own countrymen who visited the Papal States has declared: "Liberty is unknown in Rome." The most absolute despotism on the one hand and the most abject submission on the other, were seen on every side.

W. J. Stillman, who was Consul at Rome from 1861 to 1865, and who affirms that he saw, in official and private capacity, as much as any artisan could see of the government, when speaking of it, says :

" It was simply the most *atrocious* in existence except that of Louis Napoleon Bonaparte. Its traditions were as old as its authority, and the system of repression and espionage quite worthy of St. Petersburgh. Not to speak of vague and general complaints, I know that spies were placed at the doors of the places of Protestant worship, to see if any Romans went in, and that one friend of mine, a surgeon in the French hospital, was arrested for having waited on his wife (an English woman) and carried at night to the prison of the Holy Office, (the euphonic for the inquisition,) where he was menaced with severe punishment if he not only did not abstain from courtesies to Protestantism, but compel his wife to leave the Anglican Communion and enter the Roman, and he finally escaped from them by an appeal to French protection as an employe.

" The brother of one of my most intimate friends was arrested in his bed at night, carried off by officers of the Holy Office, and never heard of again, until years after, when a released prisoner came to tell the survivor that his brother had died in the prison with him, and was buried in the earth of the dungeon.

"Another of my friends, Castellani, the jeweler, was under so severe police surveillance that for several years he had not dared walk in the street with any of his friends, and when his father died, the body was taken possession of by the police at the door of the house, the coffin surrounded by a detachment of officials, carried to the church, and the next day buried, all tokens of respect to the deceased being forbidden, and all participation in the services by his friends. He and his sons were Liberals in opinion.

"The system of terrorism was such that liberal Romans dared meet only in public, and never permitted a stranger to approach them in conversation. I never dared enter the house of a Roman friend for fear of bringing on him a domiciliary visit. * * *

"I can conceive no system of torture worse than this terrible espionage, under which every patriotic Roman lay fearful of his own breath—one scarcely daring to speak to another except in tropes and innuendoes. They suffered the penalty of crime for the *wish* merely to be free. Had it not been for the system of counter-espionage kept up by the Roman Committee on the Government, no Liberal could have lived in Rome. When suspected, they generally had warning by their own spies."

No government in Europe was so oppressive as that of Rome, and no other so hated by its subjects. However much the Pope might have been reverenced as the head of the Church, he certainly was feared and utterly detested as a civil ruler. Foreign bayonets alone kept him in power. As soon as these were removed, the people rose as one man, and by the potency of the ballot-box hurled him from his throne. Never was there a revolution more harmonious, complete, and unanimous. *Fifty thousand* votes were polled against him, and but *fifty* for him, a thousand to one. Romanists in the very shadow of St. Peter's, who know all about the Pope, have swept away by their own act the foul despotism that has crushed them through all the past. No wonder there is rejoicing among the priest-ridden and ill-governed people of that ancient city. Says Dr. Nelson in a recent letter from Rome : " The citizens say they can breathe more freely than ever before, and begin already to know what is meant by freedom of thought and speech."

There is, however, another fact in this connection that has a direct bearing upon this question. On the 4th of December following the election held by the liberated people of Rome, the Catholic archbishops, bishops, and priests of these United States, in the most public and formal manner, entered their solemn protest against this popular election, against free suffrage, against the Romans choosing their own rulers, against those principles that lie at the very foundation of our government. They expressed no sympathy with a down-trodden and oppressed people that had gloriously thrown off the galling yoke that oppressed them, but sympathy with the tyrant who had justly been deposed by the popular will of the people, expressed in regular form, with a unanimity most overwhelming in its significance—sympathy with a civil power, that has been not only a scandal to the Church of Rome, but to the nineteenth century, for its despotic severity. Can we conceive of a more inconsistent and humiliating spectacle than that exhibited by these foreigners, who have come here to enjoy our free institutions, entering their protest against democratic principles and popular rights? Who can fail to see, in the light of the above, that we have, in the Romish hierarchy in the United States, a most determined combination against all of those institutions which are our glory and our boast?

Said Father Preston, of New York, in an address delivered on the 27th of November last: " Once admit that the foundation of civil authority rests in the will of the people—that men may change the form of government, and you have chaos instead of order." And again : " The right of a sovereign cannot be taken from him without a violation of the law of Almighty God." This condemns the whole of the foundation upon which our free institutions rest. According to this, our forefathers committed a great crime in rebelling against George III.; and further, our government has no right to exist, and ought to be overthrown. By the dissemination of such opinions, this Romish politico-ecclesiastical organization, which is foreign in its origin, in its sympathies, and in its interests, is not only importing foreign vassals who are ready to do its bidding, but is also sending a most destructive anti-republican influence throughout our land. What is the present *Syllabus* of Pius IX. but the reiteration of despotic assumptions? There is scarcely a single fundamental postulate of the liberalism, advanced civilization, and political reforms of the nineteenth century, that it does not unqualifiedly condemn.

Such is the doctrine of Popery, and such are the teachings of her priests and bishops in our midst to-day,—teachings that directly tend to undermine the entire fabric of our institutions.

With all these facts before us, can any one fail to understand that the policy of Rome is now what it ever has been, despotic in theory, in principle, and in practice! If she does not now tyrannize over governments as formerly, it is simply because she has not the power. She has never renounced the right to depose rulers, and release subjects from their allegiance at pleasure. Hardly thirty years have passed since she struggled hard to revive the horrors of the Inquisition in Spain; and recent events show what she would do in the United States if she could.

CHAPTER XXIII.

Romanism an Intolerant and Persecuting Power.

THE history of Papal Rome is not only a history of a complete despotism, but also a history of the most bigoted intolerance and cruel persecution, that has been remorselessly waged by her, when she has chanced to have the power, against all such as dared to worship God according to the dictates of their own consciences instead of according to the dictum of Rome. Nor should it be forgotten that this spirit of persecution, which has made the earth drunk with the blood of the saints, is strictly in accordance with her avowed principles. These are clearly taught in her Canon Law, which is made up of the writings of the Fathers, the decrees of Councils, and the bulls and decretals of the Popes. This law is based on the assumption that the authority of the Pope extends over all, even Protestants as well as Papists, and that every officer of the Church is bound to administer discipline on this basis. Cardinal Bellarmine declared that the Pope "hath a full power over the whole world, both in ecclesiastical and civil affairs, and to question it was a detestable heresy. A Bull of Pope Boniface closes with these words: "Since such is our pleasure, who by divine permission rule the world."

These absurd pretensions and groundless assumptions have led to the establishment of the most diabolical system of persecution toward all whom they have designated as heretics, that ever saw the sun. The fifth Council of Toledo, Can. 3, says:

"We the Holy Council, promulge this sentence or decree, pleasing to God, that whosoever hereafter shall succeed to the kingdom, shall not mount the throne till he has sworn, among other oaths, *to permit no man to live in his kingdom who is not a Catholic.* And if, after he has taken the reins of government he shall violate this promise, let him be *anathema maranatha* in the sight of the eternal God, and become fuel for the eternal fire."

The Council of Lateran, under Innocent III., decreed that the secular power under Papal control should be required to take the following oath:

"That they will endeavor, with all their might, to exterminate from every part of their dominions, all heretical subjects, universally, that are marked out to them by the Church. But if any temporal lord, being required and admonished by the Church, shall neglect to purge his land from this heretical filthiness, he shall be tied up in the band of excommunication by the metropolitan and his com-provincial bishops. And if he shall neglect to make satisfaction within a year, it shall be signified to the

Pope, that he may from that time pronounce the subjects *absolved from allegiance to him*, and expose his territories to be seized on by Catholics, who, expelling heretics, shall possess the country without contradiction."

Here the most relentless and heart-sickening persecution is not only recommended, but enjoined by threats and serious penalties. And let it be understood that every canon of this Lateran Council has been endorsed by the Council of Trent.

Innocent IV., in 1254, abolished the distinction between heretics and believers in the heretics, and adjudged them both to the same torments. He also founded a confraternity of crusaders expressly to defend the inquisitors against the effects of popular indignation. Urban IV., in 1262, further provided that to prevent scandal the testimony of the witnesses against heretics was not to be taken in the presence of the accused, nor their names divulged to them. Also that the processes were to be conducted without formality, or the "row" (*strepitus*) of ordinary courts, where the pleading of advocates was permitted. Clement IV., in 1265, added a provision that any one might take a heretic, and seize his goods to his own use. Nicholas III., in 1280, added a sentence of excommunication against any layman who, either in public or in private, disputed on the Catholic faith, and decreed that if after the emancipation of any person from serfdom his father should become a heretic, the emancipation should be void, and the son should become a serf again. When, in 1486, the magistrates of Brixen refused to burn heretics, on the ground that heresy was only an ecclesiastical offence, Innocent VIII. excommunicated them unless they carried out the sentences of the inquisitors, without appeal, within six days.

This boasted supremacy, that has been so frequently asserted by fire and sword, and which has worn out the saints of the Most High, is steadily inculcated and enjoined upon all that are directly entrusted with the interest of the hierarchy. The persecution of heretics was one of the solemn obligations assumed by every Jesuit at his consecration. This order, established by Pope Paul III., and invested with functions and prerogatives superior to bishops and even archbishops, that they might the more efficiently do the will of the Pope, were inducted into their office by the following oath :

"I do renounce and disown any allegiance as due to any heretical king, prince, or state, named Protestants, or obedience to any of their inferior magistrates or officers. I do further declare that the doctrine of the Church of England, of the Calvinist, Huguenots and others of the name of Protestants, to be damnable, and they themselves are damned and to be damned that will not forsake the same. I do further declare that I will help, assist and advise all or any of his Holiness' agents in any place wherever I shall be—in England, Scotland, Ireland, or in any other territory or kingdom I shall come to; and do my utmost to extirpate the heretical Protestants' doctrine, and to destroy all their pretended powers, regal or otherwise. I do further promise and declare, that notwithstanding I am dispensed with to assume any religion heretical for the propagation of Mother Church's interest, to keep secret and private all her agents' counsels from time to time, as they intrust me, and not to divulge, directly or indirectly, by word, writing, or circumstance whatever, but to execute all what shall be proposed, given in charge, or discovered unto me by you, my ghostly father, or by any of this sacred convent. All of which I, A. B., do swear by the blessed Trinity and blessed Sacrament, which I am now to receive, to perform, and on my part to keep inviolably. And do call the heavenly and glorious host of heaven to witness these, my real intentions, and to keep this my oath. In testimony hereof I take this most holy and blessed Sacrament of the Eucharist, and witness the same further with my hand and seal in the face of this holy convent."[*]

The same persecuting spirit is distinctly inculcated in the obligations imposed, and the vows assumed by the subordinate officers of the Church: "Heretics, schismatics and rebels against the same our lord (the Pope) and his successors, I will persecute and fight against to the utmost of my power." And lest an oath should be disregarded, it is provided "that if a bishop shall have been negligent or remiss in

[*] Jesuit's oath, as quoted by Usher.

purging his diocese of heretical pravity, as soon as this is made apparent by sure evidence, he shall be deposed from his episcopal office, and in his place shall be substituted a fit person who will and can confound the heretical pravity."*

Here the oath of consecration makes it the solemn duty of every bishop to "persecute and fight against heretics and schismatics to the utmost of his power." And what has been the terrible effects of this oath, let the millions that Rome has destroyed by fire and sword answer. It has converted her bishops into cold-hearted tyrants, more resembling the cruel and bloodthirsty Nero than the followers of Jesus. They have under the most solemn circumstances *pledged* themselves to persecute.

Is it, therefore, strange that under the inspiration of this persecuting spirit her annals should be filled with blood? That the heart should sicken at the sad recital of the tortures, sufferings and deaths of the vast multitudes that have fallen under her displeasure, until the very earth has been reddened with human gore from her hands?

Although this can never justify, it however accounts for the terrible persecution that was waged by Rome in the thirteenth century against the Waldenses. This people, who in-

* Form of oath at the consecration of a bishop in the Roman Pontifical, as quoted by Murray. Kirwin's Letters to Taney, p. 219.

habited the valley of Piedmont, would not give up their Bibles, nor acknowledge the claims of the Pope. These were their only offences. But for these they were declared heretics, and adjudged worthy of death. Castelnan was sent by the Pope as his legate, to superintend and carry on the bloody crusade against them. About three hundred thousand men were raised for this horrible purpose. The first outburst of their fury was on the town of Bezieres, which contained a population of about sixty thousand souls. The legate gave up the town to pillage, and the people to slaughter. "But how," said one of his officers, "can we distinguish the Catholic from the heretic?" The legate replied, "Kill all; the Lord will know his own." And, awful to relate, every being was slain, and the town consumed by fire!

All this, however, was only the beginning of the sorrows of that people. For nearly fifty years was this appalling carnage continued. "Battle followed battle," says Murry; "city was burned after city; valley was entered after valley, until the rugged yet fair heritage of this pious and simple people was converted into a howling wilderness—until a million of their number, under the sabre and tread of the minions of Popery, were made to bite the dust!" Morland, envoy of Cromwell to Turin, in addressing the Duke of Savoy, after reciting a list of barbarities, says: "What need I mention more, though I could reckon up very many cruelties of the same kind, if I were not astonished at the very thought of them! If all the tyrants of all time and ages were alive again, they would be ashamed when they should find that they had contrived nothing in comparison with these things that might be reputed barbarous and inhuman. Heaven itself seems astonished with the crimes of men, and the very earth to blush, being discolored with the gore and blood of so many innocent persons."

In France, the Vaudois of Province suffered from the hands of Papists very much in the same manner. On the 12th of April, 1545, "An execrable carnage began. The Vaudois were surprised and massacred as in a chase of wild beasts, their houses were burnt, their harvest despoiled, their trees torn up, their wells filled, their bridges destroyed. All was fire and blood; and the peasants of the neighboring regions going with the murderers, completed the remains of the devastation.* The men were hacked to pieces; houses were filled with women. Those attempting to escape were driven back, or butchered. The priests, who were the leaders in this infernal work, blessed the murderers, and told them to give no quarters. Many of the Vaudois fled to the mountains for

* G. De Felice's History of the Persecution of Prot. in France, p. 63.

safety, where great numbers died of starvation. Many in their extremity begged that they might have the privilege of leaving everything to their enemies, except their under-clothes, &c., &c.*

Their only crime, for which they thus suffered the loss of all things, was, that they were Protestants, and as such were worshiping God according to their own convictions. But, for this, however, they were adjudged guilty of heresy by Romanists, and doomed to destruction.

And let it be remembered, that these horrible scenes of blood and carnage at which the mind is horrified at their bare recital, were not the result of the fanatical ravings of a few unauthorized individuals. They were the result of a settled policy that had its centre in Rome; that was directed and stimulated, nay, urged by the head of the Romish Church. Pope Paul IV., in a Bull issued in the sixteenth century, affirms and decrees the following:

" I. Considering that the Roman Pontiff possesses the plenitude of power over every realm and every nation, that he alone upon earth, judges all and is judged by no one whomsoever.

II. We *renew all sentences of excommunication which have been directed against heretics, of whatsoever con-*

* Ibid, p. 69.

dition, were they Bishops, Patriarchs, or Popes, were they Kings or Emperors.

III. But since spiritual penalties are not sufficient, we, in the plenitude of the apostolic power, sanction, establish, *decree and define* by the present Constitution, which shall be *forever* in force, that all persons, Bishops, Cardinals, and others, Princes, Kings, or Emperors, who shall be convicted of schism or heresy, shall, over and above the aforesaid spiritual penalties, incur by the very fact, and without other judicial proceeding, the loss of all honor, of all power, of all authority, of every principality, dukedom, royalty, empire, and shall be forever deprived and incapable of resuming them. But furthermore, they are to be held as '*relapsed*,' as if condemned for the second time, as if, already convicted of heresy, they had already abjured and then fallen into it again. Furthermore, they are to be given over to the secular arm in order to be punished by the penalties of the law, except that, when truly penitent they are to be by the clemency and benignity of the Holy See, committed to a monastery to do penance there upon *bread and water for life*. And they are to be otherwise regarded as relapsed heretics by all men of every grade. They are to be treated as such, shunned as such, and deprived of every *consolation of humanity.*"*

For the purpose of carrying out in the most efficient manner such cruel and bloody edicts as the above, various expedients were adopted. But nothing contributed so largely toward the utter extermination of Protestants or heretics, as they were called, as the "Holy Inquisition" as it was termed, which was organized as far

---

* Father Gratry, as quoted in the *Christian World*, Aug., 1870.

back as the thirteenth century, but which attained its greatest efficiency in Spain, as established by Pope Alexander VI. This was one of the most cruel and terrible systems of persecution ever known, and was soon extended to other countries.

"The Dominican Torquemada," says Motley, "was the first Moloch to be placed upon this pedestal of blood and fire, and from that day forward the 'holy office' was almost exclusively in the hands of that band of brothers. In the eighteen years of Torquemada's administration *ten thousand two hundred and twenty* individuals were *burned alive, ninety-seven thousand three hundred and twenty-one* punished with infamy, confiscation of property, or perpetual imprisonment, so that the total number of families destroyed by this one friar alone, amounted *to one hundred and fourteen thousand four hundred and one*. In course of time the jurisdiction of office was extended. It taught the savages of India and America to shudder at the name of Christianity. The fear of its introduction froze the earliest heretics of Italy, France and Germany into orthodoxy. It was a court owing allegiance to no temporal authority, superior to all tribunals. It was a branch of monks without appeal, having its familiars in every house, diving into the secrets of every fireside, judging and executing its horrible deeds without responsibility. It condemned, not deeds, but *thoughts*.

It affected to descend into individual conscience, and to punish the crimes which it pretended to discover. Its process was reduced to a horrible simplicity. It arrested on suspicion, *tortured* till confession, and then punished by *fire*. Two witnesses, and those to separate facts, were sufficient to consign the victim to a loathsome dungeon.

Here he was sparingly supplied with food, forbidden to speak, or even sing, to which pastime it could hardly be thought he would feel much inclination, and then left to himself till famine and misery should break his spirit. When that time was supposed to have arrived he was examined. Did he confess and forswear his heresy, whether actually innocent or not, he might then assume the sacred shirt, and escape with the confiscation of all his property? Did he persist in the avowal of his innocence, two witnesses sent him to the stake, one witness to the rack. He was informed of the testimony against him, but never confronted with the witness. That accuser might be his son, father, or the wife of his bosom, for all were enjoined, under the death penalty, to inform the inquisitors of every suspicious word which might fall from their nearest relatives. The indictment being thus supported, the prisoner was tried by torture. *The rack was the court of justice;* the criminal's only advocate was his fortitude, for the nominal counsellor, who was permitted no communication with the prisoner, and was furnished neither with documents nor the power to procure evidence, was a puppet, aggravating the lawlessness of the proceedings by the mockery of legal forms. The torture took place at midnight, in a gloomy dungeon, dimly lighted by torches. The victim—whether man, matron, or tender virgin—was stripped naked, and stretched upon the wooden bench. Water, weights, fires, pulleys, screws, all the apparatus by which the sinews could be strained without cracking, the bones crushed without breaking, and the body racked exquisitely without giving up the ghost, were now put into operation. The executioner, enveloped in a black robe from head to foot, with his eyes glaring through holes cut in the hood which muffled his face, practiced successively all the forms of torture which the devilish ingenuity of the monks had invented. The imagination sickens when striving to keep pace with these dreadful realities. Those who wish to indulge their curiosity concerning the details of the system may easily satisfy themselves at the present day. The flood of light which has been poured upon the subject more than justifies the horror and the rebellion of the Netherlanders. The period during which torture might be inflicted from day to day was unlimited in duration. It could only be terminated by confession; so that the scaffold was the sole refuge from the rack. Individuals have borne the torture and the dungeon *fifteen* years, and have been burned at the stake at last.

Execution followed confession, but the number of condemned prisoners was allowed to accumulate, that a multitude of victims might grace each gala day. The *auto-de-fé* was a solemn festival. The monarch, the high functionaries of the land, the reverend clergy, the populace regarded it as an inspiring and delightful recreation. When the appointed morning arrived, the victim was taken from his dungeon. He was then attired in a yellow robe without sleeves, like a herald's coat, embroidered all over with black figures of devils. A large conical paper mitre was placed upon his head, upon which was represented a human being in the midst of flames, surrounded by imps. His tongue was then painfully gagged, so that he could neither open nor shut his mouth. After he was thus accoutered, and just as he was leaving his cell, a breakfast, consisting of every delicacy, was placed before him, and he was urged with ironical politeness to satisfy his hunger. He was then led into the public square. The procession was formed with great pomp. It was headed by the little school children, who were immediately followed by the band of prisoners, each attired in the horrible yet ludicrous manner described. Then came the magistrates and nobility, the prelates and other dignitaries of the Church, the holy inquisitors, with their familiars and officials, followed, all on horseback, with the blood-red flag of the 'sacred office' waving above them, blazoned upon either side with the portraits of Alexander and of Ferdinand, the pair of brothers who had established the institution. After the procession came the rabble. When all had reached the neighborhood of the scaffold, and had been arranged in order, a sermon was preached to the assembled multitude. It was filled with laudations of the inquisition, and with blasphemous revilings against the condemned prisoners. Then the sentences were read to the individual victims. Then the clergy chanted the fifty-first Psalm, the whole vast throng uniting in one tremendous *miserere*. If a priest happened to be among the culprits, he was now stripped of the canonicals which he had hitherto worn, while his hands, lips and shaven crown were scraped with a bit of glass, by which process the oil of his consecration was supposed to be removed. He was then thrown into the common herd. Those of the prisoners who were reconciled, and those whose execution was not yet appointed, were now separated from the others. The rest were compelled to mount a scaffold, where the executioner stood ready to conduct them to the fire. The inquisitors then delivered them into his hands, with an ironical request that he would deal with them tenderly, and without blood-letting or injury. Those who remained steadfast to the last were then burned at the stake; they who, in the last extremity, renounced their faith, were strangled before being thrown into the flames.

Such was the Spanish inquisition—technically so called. It was, according to the biographer of Philip the Second, a heavenly remedy, a guardian angel of Paradise, a lion's den in which Daniel and other just men could sustain no injury, but in which perverse sinners were torn to pieces. It was a tribunal superior to all human law, without appeal, and certainly owing no allegiance to the powers of earth or heaven. No rank, high or humble, was safe from its jurisdiction. The royal family were not sacred nor the pauper's hovel. Even death afforded no protection. The holy office invaded the prince in his palace and the beggar in his shroud. The corpses of dead heretics were mutilated and burned. The inquisitors preyed upon carcasses and rifled graves."*

Is it possible to conceive of a more diabolical institution? Could the Devil himself have invented a more infernal system than the ever-to-be execrated Inquisition? And yet this abomination, this Juggernaut, was instituted and managed by Romanists in the cause of Popery for the purpose of crushing out every vestige of free thought and conscientious deviation from the corrupt teachings of that Church.

When Rome kindled the fires of persecution against the Protestants of Holland, the inquisition was transferred to that country, as it would do its bloody work more efficiently than any other system. It accordingly set about the business of subjugation and extermination with a will. In these Netherlands in 1568 some "three millions" of men, women, and children were declared to be fit subjects for the slaughter. The work of torture and butchery now commenced in earnest. The cries of the help-

* Motley's His. of Dutch Rep. v. 1, p. 322—26.

less and the groans of the dying were heard on every side. The most summary forms of condemnation were adopted. The culprit was denied every opportunity of defence. The only thing certain was condemnation. Then came the pulleys, screws or fire. Various were the modes of torture and the means of destruction.

That the reader may form some further idea of their nature, we subjoin the account of the execution of Bertrand le Blas by the Inquisition:

"He was dragged on a hurdle, with his mouth closed with an iron gag, to the market-place. Here his right hand and foot were burned and twisted off between two red-hot irons. His tongue was then torn out by the roots, and because he still endeavored to call upon the name of God, the iron gag was again applied. With his arms and legs fastened together behind his back, he was then hooked by the middle of his body to an iron chain and made to swing to and fro, over a slow fire, till he was entirely roasted. His life lasted almost to the end of these ingenious tortures, but his fortitude lasted as long as life."*

Mr. Motley, after describing various other cases and methods of destruction to which these people were subjected by Popery, says:

"This was the treatment to which thousands and tens of thousands had been subjected in the provinces. Men, women and children were burned, and their cinders

* Motley's His. etc., v. 1. p. 335.

thrown away, for idle words against Rome, spoken years before, for praying alone in the closet, for not kneeling to a wafer when they met it in the streets, for thoughts to which they had never given utterance, but which on enquiry they were too honest to deny."*

Now what had these heretics done that they should be thus slaughtered without mercy? Why, they had presumed to think for themselves, to worship God according to the Scriptures as they honestly understood them; they had refused to affirm their belief in the infallibility of the Romish Church, and that there was no salvation outside of her communion; they had protested against the invocation of saints, transubstantiation, the adoration of the host, the worship of images, etc. These were their leading crimes, for which they were hurled from all the endearments of society and visited with the confiscation of their estates, arrests, imprisonments, excruciating pain and death. But why should they have been put to death? If that, however, were deemed necessary, why must they be tortured? Why must pulleys, weights, screws and fires be called into requisition to strain, tear, crack, crush and burn the muscles, sinews, tendons, ligaments, nerves and bones of their poor victims until life was destroyed by slow and ingenious torture? And why, in the name of all that is

* Ibid, p. 339.

sacred, should cruel mockery be added to their sufferings by their persecutors when, handing them over to the civil magistrate to carry out the sentence of death, they implore him "for the love of God, and in regard to piety and mercy, and of their mediation, to free this miserable person from all danger of death, or mutilation of members"—when they have handed the person over to him for this very purpose, and at the same time would burn the magistrate if he should dare to refuse to carry out their sentences! Can any one conceive of more flagrant hypocrisy and disgusting cant, than this lying ceremony? Such cruelty and hypocritical conduct would far better become the savages of our western wilds than the ecclesiastics of even the Church of Rome.

About in keeping with the foregoing in cruelty and brutality was the horrible massacre of St. Batholomew, in France, in 1572. The houses of the Protestants were all marked—the dwellings of the Papists were supplied with torches—badges and arms were furnished the assassins. Everything being thus secretly arranged, at midnight the alarm-bell was rung from St. Germain. This was the signal for the murderers to commence the work of slaughter. Immediately, as if by magic, the Tuilleries, the Palais, the public places, the large edifices and the streets of Paris were brilliantly illuminated to light up the pathway of these cut-throats to the houses of their victims. The terrible carnage now commenced with untold fury in every street and lane of the city. The shouts of these assassins to each other to let no one escape, and the wailing of men, the shrieking of women and children as they were falling under the blows of their murderers, made the night more hideous than words can portray. But the slaughter ended not with the night. For seven days it raged with fiendish fury throughout the city. From the capital it extended to the provinces, where, for two months, the horrid work went on, until eighty-five thousand Protestants were slain. The tidings of this infernal slaughter, that spread horror and consternation throughout the civilized world, was received at Rome with thanksgiving. Cannon were fired from its walls with public rejoicings. A *Te Deum* was sung, at which the Pope and his court attended; a medal was struck to commemorate the event, and a picture of the massacre was put up in the Pope's palace to commemorate the triumph of the Church over Protestanism.

The persecutions of the Protestants in Ireland by the Papists in 1641 was even worse than the preceding. The chief actor in this awful tragedy was the Romish Bishop of Down. It is a matter of history that on the Sabbath preceding the commencement of the massacre the Romish priests, after celebrating Mass, sent out their communicants with the command to kill the Protestants and seize their property. The plan of attack and mode of procedure had all been secretly arranged. The 23rd of October was fixed upon as the day upon which their hellish work was to begin. On that fatal morning the Protestants arose from their beds in perfect ignorance of the terrible fate that awaited them. They were soon overwhelmed with amazement to see their nearest neighbors, with whom they lived in friendly intercourse, approaching them with the weapons of death. In vain did they plead for life. No mercy was shown to sex, age or condition. Resistance was hopeless amid such armed numbers. If they escaped from one, it was only to fall a victim to the fury of others. No asylum was respected. The blood flowed upon every side. The air was filled all day long with the wailings of the dying. Some were stabbed, some were shot, some were hung, some were drowned, some were torn to pieces by dogs, some were hewn to pieces with axes, while many who shut themselves up in their houses as the best means of safety, had their dwellings set on fire, and so perished in the flames. Thus the horrid work went on until two hundred thousand Protestants were destroyed.

CHAPTER XXIV.

Popish Persecutions of Bible Readers in Madeira.

The system of Romanism is, from its very nature, necessarily a system of intolerance and persecution. Many lose sight of this essential characteristic of Romanism, from the fact, that in the United States they have seen no such persecution by Papists as has been alleged to have taken place in other countries and at other times, and they are therefore ready to conclude that these charges are in whole or in part unfounded, or that Popery has changed. It should, however, be borne in mind that the Church of Rome dare not at present in this country attempt to carry out her system—she dare not now outrage public opinion, and trample our laws under her feet. They are yet largely in the minority of the population of our country, and consequently, such a course would be suicidal. It would tend to awaken our people to a sense of the danger that threatens them, and thereby defeat the very object they have in view. They understand as well as any body else, that to succeed here at present, they must do in some measure as Protestants do, in showing kindness to other denominations. Hence, we can know nothing comparatively of Popery by our acquaintance with it here. If we would see and understand its character and workings, we must go to other lands where it is in the ascendency. There it not only can suppress the circulation of the Scriptures, and punish Bible readers, but generally does so. This persistent determination of Rome to prevent the circulation and reading of the Scriptures to the extent of her power, is very clearly illustrated in her persecution of Bible readers in the Island of Madeira, from 1843 to 1846.

In 1838, Dr. Kalley, a minister of the Free Church of Scotland, moved to Madeira, with the design of making it his future home. Although the Roman Catholic religion was the religion of the Island, and priests were there in abundance, he found the inhabitants in the most deplorable and almost incredible ignorance of the word of God. "*None of them,*" says Dr. Kalley, "*had in their possession a copy of the Scriptures. The people were not only destitute of the Bible, but it was a rare case to find any one who knew there was a book that contained a history of Jesus Christ.* That many of them had never heard of such a book until they heard it from him."

Dr. Kalley, who at first could scarcely believe such astounding declarations; such incredible ignorance among a people who professed to be Christians, resolved to dissipate this gross moral darkness, by supplying them with the word of God. For this purpose, and in order not to offend the authorities of the Island, or the Romish hierarchy, he procured a supply of Portuguese Bibles, which had been translated by Antonia Pereira, a Romish priest, and which had been sanctioned by the Queen and the Romish Patriarch of Portugal. These Bibles were circulated among the people and were read, by such as could read, with an astonishing interest. As many who were hungering and thirsting after the word of life, were unable to read, meetings were appointed at private places where they assembled to hear some one of their number read aloud for the edification of the rest. Schools were also established by Dr. Kalley to teach the art of reading the word.

In this way the blessed work went on silently, yet surely, without any open outbreak from the bishops or priests until 1843. During this period many had learned to read, and Bible readers had greatly multiplied, and many had embraced its doctrines by faith, in opposition to the absurd dogmas of Rome. The growing intelligence of the people, however, became too manifest to escape observation. The priests began to be alarmed. They plainly saw that this practice of Bible reading, if continued, would result in serious injury, if not in fatal disaster to their church. It was evident their craft was in danger. As Romanism could not endure the light of Revelation, the light must be put out, or at least under a bushel. The Bible must be suppressed and its readers punished. A most vigorous course was now commenced by the bishops and priests. The Bible and Bible readers were denounced as the fruitful sources of all heresies. They declared *"the Bible was a book from hell; and should be burnt with the hands that handle it."* Bible meetings were also denounced in unmeasured terms of execration, and frequently broken up by Romish mobs led by fanatical priests. Ecclesiastical penalties speedily followed. On a day fixed upon by the Vicar-General, there was read from all the pulpits in Madeira the excommunication with the curse of Almighty God on these Bible readers. This document goes on to say, "Let no one give them fire, water, bread, or any thing that may be necessary for their support. Let no one pay them their debts. Let no one support them in any case which they may bring before a court of justice. Let all put them aside as rotten and excommunicated members, separated from the bosom and union of the Holy Mother Catholic Church, and as rebels and contumacious." It further excommunicated *ipso facto* all who did not comply with these commands—every debtor who should pay these men their just debts, every judge who should dare, in a court of law, to do them justice, every charitable person who should give them water, fire, or any thing necessary to existence.

The strong arm of the law was also invoked to assist in the horrible work of persecution. Bible readers were reported by the priests to the government, and the work of arrests and imprisonments at once commenced. "A judge and public prosecution," says Captain Tate, "with a notary and about sixty soldiers proceeded at night to the Sombo das Fayas. The houses of the Bible readers were broken open—thirty men and women were taken prisoners—most of them were bound—many of them were beaten, and some of them very severely—and their houses were given up to be sacked by the soldiers, who committed the most horrible atrocities. With scarcely any clothes on (for they had been roused from their beds by the soldiers) twenty-two of them were conveyed to Funchal—and there committed to prison. In prison *they were denied the liberty to read the word of God;* and though mass had not been performed in it for years, it was now found useful as a means of persecution, and *they were driven to mass at the point of the bayonet.*" "Here," adds the same authority, " they lay confined for more than twenty long months without a hearing."

Arrests continued to be made and the number of the imprisoned increased. In the mean time it being ascertained that Bible reading was kept up in the prison, the judge with other officers visited the jail, and " ordered all the boxes of the prisoners to be searched for Bibles; and he took away every copy of the Scriptures he could find." They went to a school supported by English charity, and took away thirty Bibles and all their Testaments. The search for Bibles in private houses and every where was prosecuted with such vigor that some concealed their Bibles in their beds, some in cellars, some in barns, some in stone walls, and some buried them in the earth.

In the mean time the persecution of the Bible readers increased. The storm thickened. Their meetings were broken up with violence. Their houses were sacked, plundered, and their furniture destroyed. To escape the fury of the priests and their minions these Protestants fled to the mountains and hid themselves in dens and caves of the earth. " On the evening of the 5th (1846,") says Dr. Kalley, " many houses were plundered by bands of marauding ruffians, and sixty or eighty of the converts were compelled to leave their homes, and pass the night in the mountains. Night after night these bands continued to repeat their desolating work; and in greater and greater numbers were the believers driven from their houses:—till on Sunday *many* hundreds of the Portuguese subjects, obnoxious to the priests, only on account of their adherence to the Gospel truth, had fled for their lives. The mob had broken open their doors, and destroyed their windows, furniture, and other property. When the work of destruction was completed in the town and neighborhood, the ruthless persecutors followed the scattered flock to the mountains, hunting them down like beasts of prey." Such of those as died or were killed were denied a burial save in the public highway. For them there was no justice, law, security, asylum, or mercy. Being pursued to the mountains, they fled from the Island by every available means. In their flight some found refuge in the West India Islands. Many in Trinidad, and some in the United States. Dr. Kalley escaped in the guise of a female while they were seeking for his life. The number that thus fled the Island to escape the fury of this storm of persecution by Papists against Bible readers was more than one thousand. Who shall tell the sum of their sufferings, their anxiety, alarm, and hunger in the mountains, their cruel separations from kindred, home and their father-land; robbed of their property, outcasts and wanderers in strange lands? And all this for what? for reading God's Revelation to man! And all this too by the professed followers of Him who said: "*Search the Scriptures.*" Was there ever greater blindness, or stranger infatuation? Has Rome changed in reference to her opposition to the Bible during the dark ages? The answer to this question is furnished by her cruel persecutions of Bible readers in Madeira, in 1846, in the middle of the 19th century.* Is it therefore strange that she should still hate Bible reading by the masses, and demand its expulsion from our schools? Let it be remembered, these Bibles circulated in Madeira were not Protestant translations. They were translated by a Romish priest, and approved by the Romish Queen and Patriarch of Portugal. And yet they were denounced as *from hell*, and committed to the flames by the priests, wherever they were found.

* See Book entitled "Facts in Madeira."

CHAPTER XXV.

Rome still a Persecutor in Spirit.

IN proof that Rome is still a persecutor in spirit, the following additional facts are presented for careful consideration :

In the first place, it is a prime dogma of Romanism, that all which the Church teaches through the approved channels of the Popes and Councils is sacred, infallible and unchangeable. Let this be distinctly understood. What she has once taught as right, must forever remain to her as right! Changes, innovations, repeals, reforms or progress, can find no admittance into the Papal system, without destroying this fundamental principle, or foundation, upon which the whole superstructure stands. "The whole of our faith," says Cardinal Pullavicini, *an infallible authority*, "rests upon one indivisible article, namely, the infallible authority of the Church. The moment, therefore, that we give up any part whatever, the whole falls; for what admits not of being divided, must evidently stand entire or fall entire."

Now from all this it is manifestly plain that all and each of these decrees, laws, precepts and practices of Popery, from the earliest ages of her history down to the present day may, with strict propriety, be brought forward as evidence of what she would do at present if she could have her own way. Her teachings of intolerance to her people; her instructions to her bishops, who still swear: "Heretics, schismatics, or rebels against our lord the Pope, or his successors, I will persecute and fight against to the utmost of my power,"—and her exhortations to kings and princes to aid her in the horrid work of slaughter, that still disgraces the pages of her textbooks—all bear unmistakable evidence that she has not changed.

"Let the secular powers be compelled, if necessary, to exterminate, to their utmost power, all the heretics denoted by the church."*

"Experience teaches that there is no other remedy for the evils but to put heretics to death."†

Again: "The blood of the heretics is not called the blood of the saints no more than the blood of thieves, mankillers, and other malefactors, for the shedding of which, by the order of justice, no commonwealth shall suffer.‡

When has Rome ever repudiated these teachings, which form no inconsiderable amount of her literature? What one of all her Popes has ever condemned the slaying of Protestants as a

* Gen. Coun. Sat. † Bellarm de Laicis, Lib. 3, c. 21.
‡ Rheim, Test., Rev. 17. 6.

righteous vindication of the truth? When, and where, has the Romish hierarchy ever deplored the horrible massacre of St. Bartholomew, or the Irish massacre of two hundred thou and Protestants, or any other wholesale butchery in which she has been engaged? Indeed, so far from this, the memory of the massacre of St. Bartholomew is preserved by a picture of that awful scene, that still hangs in one of the rooms of the Vatican of Rome, to feast the eyes of the Pope and his Cardinals.

But we are not left to draw our inferences from the bulls of Popes, and the decrees of Councils, or the bloody persecutions she has waged in former times, against all who dared to think for themselves, as to what her spirit of intolerance is at present. Although prudence and cautiousness have ever been characteristic of her utterances in this land, as to her intentions, should she ever get the power to assert her supremacy, yet such has been the confidence of success, upon the part of some of her leading officials, as has led them in part to unfold their future programme:

"Protestantism of every form has not, and never can have, any right where Catholicity is triumphant; and, therefore, we lose the breath we expend in declaiming against bigotry and intolerance, and in favor of religious liberty, or the right of any man to be of any religion as best pleases him."*

* Catholic Review, January, 1852.

No worse form of intolerance than the above was uttered by Rome during the period of her fiercest persecutions. It was this sentiment, carried out by the Romish hierarchy, that has in former times destroyed millions of the faithful. This sentiment of intolerance she tells us she holds to-day. "Religious liberty is merely endured," says Bishop O'Connor of Pittsburgh, "until the opposite can be carried into operation without peril to the Catholic world."

Rome is doing in this respect the best she can under the circumstances. No matter how much the world out-travels her, no matter in what dusty and mouldy piles her dogmas lie, no matter how her spiritual prince on the Tiber may tremble and fly, she plots as keenly as ever, and does with might and main the thing within her reach, whatever it may be. Where she has more power, she does more.

Rev. Oscar Hugo, an expelled Hungarian, preached not long since in Williamsburgh, when in speaking of the religious affairs of his country, and a Catholic concordat against Protestants, said:

"According to that concordat all marriages by Protestants were considered null and void, and the entire eleven millions were thus considered to be

IN A STATE OF ADULTERY.

A council, composed of an archbishop and four Jesuits, had power at any time to close a Protestant church. At last, that concordat was abolished and Protestants were free, but they did not retaliate, they did not close any Catholic churches. After a brief period it was re-established, and we had to submit to it again. On the 9th day of May, 1851, a council of Protestant ministers was convened in the city of Pesth, for the purpose of petitioning for a modification of it. A petition was drawn up and signed by the members of the council, and it was entrusted to a committee for presentation to the authorities. That committee, as well as the council itself, were denounced as heretics and rebels, and the Church authorities advised that they all be thrown into prison. On the 27th of May, while the most revered of the Protestant clergy of Hungary was offering up a prayer, a military force entered the church and took him and all present prisoners, because they had not received permission from the Emperor of Austria to worship God according to their consciences. They were thrown into prison and were all more or less tortured. My father, himself a minister, was sentenced to seven years' imprisonment because he was a member of the council, and he died in prison. Because I attended the council with my father, I was sentenced to perpetual banishment from my native land. That's the way Catholics respected Protestant consciences in Hungary in 1851. That's the way they would respect your consciences here if they had the power."

As we have already seen, in the Island of Madeira no longer ago than in 1846, she waged a most cruel system of persecution against those who were charged with no other crime than simply reading their Bibles and meeting for worship in private houses. For doing such things they were declared outlaws; the courts closed against them; their property confiscated; their meetings broken up; their houses plundered; harassed and persecuted, they fled to the mountains and hid themselves in dens and caves, where they suffered exceedingly from exposure and hunger, until they could escape from the Island.

In 1863, only eight years ago, the Pope concluded a Concordat with the government of Ecuador, which includes the following articles:

1. "The Catholic religion is the religion of the State; consequently the practice of any other mode of worship is *forbidden* in the Republic.

2. Every book forbidden by a bishop is confiscated by the government.

6. The government will lend the bishops its powerful aid in putting down every one who attempts to lead the faithful into the paths of error (Protestantism)."

Such is the bigotry, exclusiveness, intolerance, and persecution, that are carried out to-day by Roman Catholics in a neighboring Republic, and such would be her intolerant despotism in the United States, if she had the ability.

Less than two years ago, Cardinal Antonelli, the Prime Minister of the Pope of Rome, wrote as follows, to the Bishop of Nicaragua:

"We have lately been informed here that an attempt has been made to change the order of things hitherto existing in that republic, by publishing a programme, in which are enunciated '*freedom of education*' *and of worship*. Both these principles are not only contrary to the laws of God and of the Church, but are in contradiction with the Concordat established between the Holy See and that republic. Although we doubt not that your most illustrious and reverend lordship will do all in your power against maxims so *destructive to the Church* and to society, still we deem it by no means superfluous to stimulate your well-known zeal to see that the clergy, and above all the curates, do their duty.*

"G. CARDINAL ANTONELLI."

Here, "freedom of education and worship" are declared to be offensive to Popery and contrary to the Concordat, or the agreement that had been exacted of them by the Pope, and which it was now found necessary to hold them to, by intimidation. It is also most explicitly declared by the Cardinal that "freedom of education and worship are both *contrary* to the laws of God and the *Church*." As it respects the former, the Cardinal is unquestionably very ignorant, which is probably owing to his being opposed to Bible reading; but in reference to the latter, he undoubtedly knows whereof he affirms. The history of Rome has ever been a history of bigotry, intolerance, and cold-hearted tyranny, which is in the above extract re-affirmed by Papal authority.

By the enactment of the dogma of Papal Infallibility, the cruel and bloodthirsty decrees

* "Nicaragua Gazette" of January 1, 1870.

of Popes Innocent IV., Urban IV., Clement IV., Nicholas III., and Innocent VIII., are not only sanctioned, but declared to be just and right, and must be regarded as embodying the spirit of Rome to-day, and for all coming time.

At a recent meeting held in the City of New York, Dr. S. J. Prime, in addressing the audience, said:

"Four years ago I was in Rome, and was pleasantly associated with a Scotch clergyman, who was holding every Sabbath day a religious service in his own hired house, with a few British and American Christians. But while I was there, an order came to this Scotch preacher, telling him that he was violating the law of the city, and exposed himself to the *Inquisition ; he must stop that preaching* or the *Inquisition* would put its loving arms about him and crush him in its fatal hug. *The Inquisition was an existing institution in Rome three weeks ago;* and is it nothing to thank God for that it exists no longer? In 1848, when for a brief hour the Republicans held Rome, during the flight of this Pope, the dungeons and pit of that infernal Inquisition were opened, and out of the depths were drawn up remnants of clothing, and human bones, and long locks of human hair—woman's hair —*the ghastly relics of hapless victims of religious persecution and hate in the nineteenth century* of Christ's era."

No one need to be deceived as to the persecuting spirit of Popery. Her very element is cruelty and blood. Popery encourages, nay, commands the extermination of all heretics (Protestants), as a sacred duty wherever it may be practicable; that it is no more sin to kill heretics than to kill dogs, but that it is meritorious. The tears and groans of her victims can not be numbered. The voice of the blood of millions of martyrs to-day cry out against her from the ground. While the Lord Jesus Christ says: "If thine enemy hunger, feed him—if he thirst, give him drink, etc.;" and again, "Love your enemies, bless them that curse you, do good to them that hate you, and pray for them which despitefully use you, and persecute you." Popery has inculcated cruelty toward all who dared to think for themselves, as a virtue. She has not only decreed death to heretics as a sacred duty, but death in its most terrible forms. The fire, the rack, and various other devices of cruel torture, have been her favorite methods of procedure with those charged with heresy.

But it may be said that "its hierarchy would not be guilty of such atrocious deeds of cruelty now, and especially in the United States." That many of them would not, I have not a doubt. Many of them are not only kind and humane, but evidently in charity with all mankind. But individual excellence has nothing to do with the system, or with the doctrines and tenets of the Church. The hierarchs have long been upbraided for their intolerance and cruelty, and if they have changed in these respects, why did they not in their recent Œcumenical Council say so? Why did they not, like honest men, publicly before the world, hasten, without mental reservation or hypocrisy, to wash their bloody hands from these murderous abominations that disgrace their Church's history? The reason is plain. Rome is the same *now* as in the past. She not only neither forsakes, repents, or apologizes, for the cruel persecutions of the past, but by the decision of that Council she has, in the most solemn manner, lifted up the cruel and bloody decrees of former Popes, into the region of infallibility, thus making them an essential part of her abominable system for all time to come. Hence Rome has not changed in this respect, nor can she change, so long as this absurd dogma of Papal infallibility is suffered to disgrace her canon laws.

As an illustration of the cruel and antiChristian spirit of Rome to-day, look at the vindictiveness, the hate, and diabolical fury embodied in her *Anathema Maranatha*, which is still retained in her judicial system for use, and which is said to have been recently hurled against Victor Emanuel:

" By authority of the Almighty God, the Father, Son, and Holy Ghost; and of the holy canons; and of the undefiled Virgin Mary, mother and nurse of our Saviour; and of the celestial virtues, angels, archangels, thrones, dominions, powers, cherubims and seraphims; and of all the holy patriarchs and prophets; and of all apostles and evangelists; and of the holy innocents (who, in the sight of the Holy Lamb, are found worthy to sing the new song); and of the holy martyrs and holy confessors; and of the holy virgins; and of all the saints, together with all the holy and elect of God—we excommunicate and anathematize him, and from the threshold of the holy Church of God Almighty we sequester him, that he may be tormented in eternal, excruciating sufferings, together with Dathan and Abiram, and those who say to the Lord God, "Depart from us; we desire none of Thy ways." And as fire is quenched with water, so let the light of him be put out forevermore.

May the Father who created man curse him. May the Son who suffered for us curse him. May the Holy Ghost which was given to us in our baptism, curse him. May the Holy Cross which Christ (for our salvation triumphing over his enemies) ascended, curse him. May the Holy and Eternal Virgin Mary, Mother of God, curse him. May St. Michael, the advocate of holy souls, curse him. May all the angels and archangels, principalities and powers, and all the heavenly armies curse him. May St. John, the precursor, and St. John the Baptist, and St. Peter and St. Paul, and St. Andrew, and all other of Christ's apostles together curse him. And may the rest of his disciples and four Evangelists (who by their preaching converted the universal world), and may the holy and wonderful company of martyrs and confessors (who by their holy works are found pleading to God Almighty) curse him.

May the Choir of the Holy Virgins (who for the honor of Christ have despised the things of the world), damn him; may all the saints (who from the beginning of the world and everlasting ages are found to be beloved of God), damn him; may the heavens and the earth, and all the holy things remaining therein, damn him.

May he be damned, wherever he be, whether in the house or in the field, whether in the highway or the byway, whether in the wood or in the water, or whether in the church. May he be cursed in living and in dying, in eating and drinking, in fasting and thirsting, in slumbering and sleeping, in watching or walking, mingendo, cacando, and in blood-letting.

May he be cursed in all the faculties of his body. May he be cursed inwardly and outwardly. May he be cursed in his hair. May he be cursed in his brains. May he be cursed in the crown of his head and in his temples. In his forehead and in his ears. In his eyebrows and in his cheeks. In his jawbones and in his nostrils. In his fore teeth and in his grinders. In his lips and in his throat. In his shoulders and in his wrists. In his arms, his hands, and in his fingers.

May he be damned in his mouth, in his breast, in his heart, and in all the viscera of his body; may he be damned in his veins and in his groin, in his thighs and * * * * in his hips and in his knees, in his legs, feet and toe-nails!

May he be cursed in all the joints and articulations of his members. From the top of his head to the sole of his foot may there be no soundness in him.

May the Son of the living God, with all the glory of his majesty, curse him; and may Heaven, with all the powers that move therein, rise up against him, curse and damn him!

Amen. So be it. Amen."*

Can any one imagine a greater contrast than the spirit exhibited by Jesus Christ, who says; "Bless and curse not," and that of Popery, as set forth in the above?

* This curse, which was in use before the Reformation, may be found in Lea's Studies in Church History, page 335.

And now, in conclusion, I would remark that it seems to me that no one can fail to see that the success of Popery in our midst, according to the unqualified declarations of her authorized expounders of her principles, necessarily involves the utter extinction of Protestant liberty, and the destruction of our free institutions. Equality with Protestants she utterly abhors, and will never rest until she shall tread them in the dust. She is the same now in all essential particulars that she has been in the past—the implacable foe of civil and religious liberty—a foe that scruples not to use any means, or measures, however cruel, to compel submission to her despotic behests. And as if to indoctrinate her communicants of the nineteenth century into her spirit of intolerance and hatred toward all Protestants, and if possible to inflame their minds with the spirit of persecution toward all other sects, so that they may be ready at any time to do the bidding of their spiritual guides in any emergency, the following is read in every Romish church on Thursday before Easter: "In the name of God Almighty, Father, Son and Holy Ghost, and by the authority of the Apostles, Peter and Paul, and by our own, we excommunicate and anathematize all Hussites, Wicliffites, Lutherans, Zwinglians, Calvinists, Huguenots, Anabaptists, Trinitarians, and other apostates from the faith; and all other heretics, by whatsoever name they are called, or of whatsoever sect they may be. And also their adherents, receivers, favorers, and generally any defenders of them—as also schismatics, and those who withdraw themselves, or recede obstinately from their obedience to us or the existing Roman Pontiff."*

In this way our whole Protestant community which has so generously granted them privileges, by legal enactments, equal to their own, and who protects them in the enjoyments of those rights, is most grossly and publicly insulted yearly by this senseless and wicked practice. One would think that the baseness of the act to thus scorn and treat a benefactor, would crimson their cheeks with shame.

Of these things, as Protestants, we have a right to complain. When Romanists deem it their duty to trample down the rights of others, to denounce Protestants as heretics and schismatics, with whom they are not bound to keep faith, and who are to be endured only until they get the power to crush them; when they publicly declare themselves to be the uncompromising enemies of religious liberty, and free institutions in general, then indeed it is high time that we should awaken to the impending danger that threatens us, and to the fearful crisis that is upon us.

* Bula in Coena Domini.

www.ingramcontent.com/pod-product-compliance
Lightning Source LLC
Chambersburg PA
CBHW032101220426
43664CB00008B/1092